# INDIA
## IN THE AGE OF
# ideas

# INDIA
## IN THE AGE OF
# ideas

SELECT WRITINGS 2006-2018

# SANJEEV SANYAL

Published by Westland Publications Private Limited
61, 2nd Floor, Silverline Building, Alapakkam Main Road, Maduravoyal, Chennai 600095

Westland and the Westland logo are the trademarks of Westland Publications Private Limited, or its affiliates.

ISBN: 9789387894570

10 9 8 7 6 5 4 3 2 1

The views and opinions expressed in this work are the author's own and the facts are as reported by him, and the publisher is in no way liable for the same.

Typeset by Ram Das Lal, New Delhi, NCR
Printed at Thomson Press (India) Ltd.

*Thou art wisdom, thou art law*
*Thou art heart, our soul, our breath*
*Thou art love divine, the awe*
*In our hearts that conquers death.*

— from Bankim Chandra Chatterjee's *Vande Mataram*
(as translated by Sri Aurobindo)

# CONTENTS

## URBAN DYNAMICS

## ECONOMICS

# FOREWORD

A Complex Adaptive System (CAS) is just that—it is complex, it is adaptive and it is a system. You can't quite model it and if you are going to analyse it, you have to be inter-disciplinary in approach. In plain language, a CAS is difficult to pin down and figure out. I am aware of a CAS-type lens being used to examine diverse phenomena. But all the ones I am aware of are inanimate entities. To the best of my knowledge, CAS approaches haven't been used to vivisect animate creatures, such as human beings. A certain type of Bengali is fertile ground for CAS scrutiny. That kind of Bengali is increasingly rare, having been far more common in the nineteenth century. Though a dying breed, such a Bengali isn't completely extinct yet. Everything in the world provides intellectual stimuli to such a Bengali and you can't straitjacket the person, pin him down. Who, or why, or which, or what, is Sanjeev Sanyal? I have no idea. He is like the Akond of Swat.

He is Principal Economic Advisor in Ministry of Finance.

Therefore, he shapes India's economic policy formulation and writes columns on economic developments, for general and business papers. He has written extensively on urban affairs and urban planning (including for books I have edited). He has also occasionally written (I think it is occasional) on environmental matters. He has dabbled in financial markets. He has spent several years of his life in the well-organised and less chaotic environment of Singapore, where the streets are lined with trees, but no birds chirp from those trees (outside Jurong Bird Park). He has written excellent books (more than one) on India's history and geography. More recently, he has also produced a collection of short stories. There is a reading interest for fiction (mentioned in an interview in this collection) straddling Ernest Hemingway and Amish Tripathi. Hence, Sanjeev is a member of that extinct tribe, the nineteenth century babu of Bengal renaissance vintage with an insatiable intellectual curiosity that can't be straitjacketed and hemmed in with labels. (The Bengali babu would have drawn a line at Taekwondo though, also mentioned in that interview.)

This is a collection of that Bengali babu's articles and columns. As is only to be expected, the pieces are written well and form an eclectic mix of economics, history (in Sanjeev's writings, geography is woven into history), culture and urban issues. More specifically, they have been segregated under three heads of History & Culture, Urban Dynamics and Economics. Why does one write a column? There can be multiple responses to that question. I have a point of view and I want that to be communicated to the rest of the world, perhaps so as to influence policy (or defend it), or engage in a debate. With that motive, columns are often triggered by a news event. Once that event has passed into oblivion, the column is no longer topical and loses relevance. The utility of compiling and publishing such columns in book form is questionable, apart of course from the questionable motive of pandering to the ego. The loss of topicality is understandably a function of the time lag between the column and the book being published and I have read compilations where that time lag has been as much as three decades. Sanjeev's columns on economics, included in this volume, are responses to immediate events. Thankfully, the time lag isn't much and readers will form an understanding about how the Principal Economic Advisor views such matters. An insider view is being communicated outside. Personally, I found the articles under the Urban Dynamics head more absorbing. Yet another reason for writing a column is a desire to learn. Every column-writer, if the person takes the job seriously, spends time on 'research' and thinking. Urban dynamics is an issue on which Sanjeev has thought, and written, for a long time. His thoughts have crystallised and there is originality in what he says. He has that USP. (On economics there will be four, though not forty, others who will say similar things.) Consequently, the CAS argument is much more convincing for this head. For History & Culture, where there is some repetition with his earlier books, I think Sanjeev Sanyal is still thinking, reflecting and pondering. The CAS idea is still a glimmer, in the distance. It will eventually crystallise, but in a subsequent book.

I suspect most readers don't know Sanjeev Sanyal also writes poetry. Unfortunately, there are no poems in this collection. Therefore,

*I read this book with pleasure*
*The particulars are not the true measure.*
*Whether you beg, buy or steal,*
*This book is a good deal –*
*There is much in it to treasure.*

Bibek Debroy
24 October 2018

# INTRODUCTION

This is a collection of articles and columns that I wrote over the course of a decade or so. Given my current job, there was a temptation to skew the selection in favour of economics, but we eventually opted for a more eclectic mix, ranging from economics, and urban design to history, culture and religion. Neat silos may be useful for pedagogical purposes, but the real world does not function in separate compartments.

I am fortunate that I have enjoyed a personal and professional life that has been rich with varied experiences. I have worked in different fields, lived in many cities in India and abroad, and travelled extensively for work and pleasure. The one thing I have learned from these experiences is that the most interesting things about the world derive from the complex and unpredictable interactions between different aspects of human activity. I have tried to reflect upon these in this collection.

## A PHILOSOPHICAL FRAMEWORK

Despite the range of topics I wade into, there is a philosophical framework that underlies much of my writing. As I have pointed out in many of my books and articles, I am specifically interested in fields of enquiry relating to Complex Adaptive Systems (CAS). What are these? Think of them as ecosystems made up of diverse factors and players who constantly interact with each other in multiple, often unpredictable ways. Unlike Newtonian systems, Complex Adaptive Systems are constantly evolving, being buffeted by shocks and influencing each other in non-linear ways. There are many examples of such systems—economies, financial markets, cities, climate systems, the English language, ecological systems and, as I argue in the first essay in this collection, Hinduism.

Complex systems can be somewhat chaotic, but they are not as random as they may appear at a first glance. Some outcomes are more likely than the others, and the interlinkages can have patterns/cycles. The English language may have many quirks and is constantly in a state of flux, but it does have a rough framework of common usages and vocabulary. The same can be said of cities and financial markets.

More importantly, the complexity framework provides a better sense of the contingent nature of historical evolution, and is a better explanation of seemingly improbable sequences of events that characterise the real world. Once a turn is taken, no matter how unlikely ex ante, it is now hardwired and impacts all subsequent events. This is called 'path-dependence' and a small change in direction can get radically amplified over time.

Moreover, a reversing of circumstances does not take you back to the origin. Thus, even if one were to perfectly reverse the factors that led to the development of a language or a city, one would not end up back where it all started. Thus, even if we were to reverse British history perfectly— no easy task—the English language would not go back to being medieval Anglo-Saxon. Mumbai will not go back to being seven swampy islands even if the Portuguese royals were somehow persuaded to take back their dowry. The readers will notice how this is fundamentally different from the relatively easy reversibility of a Newtonian system.

One of the consequences of using the CAS framework is that it can often lead to very different analytical outcomes than those derived from traditional intellectual frameworks. For instance, there is no 'equilibrium' to which economies and financial markets will naturally gravitate. There is nothing 'natural' about the so-called natural interest rates or unemployment rates that economists use to recommend policy action. Similarly, cities are seen as evolving organisms that will always defy rigid, long-term masterplans. Languages that thrive are not those with well-defined vocabularies and grammar (as language purists often try to impose), but those that add new usages, words, and literature with ease.

Welcome to a world of organic evolution, 'butterfly effects', where small changes can have a big impact and vice-versa; where the whole is not the sum of parts; and where human interventions always risk unintended consequences.

One would imagine that it would be natural to think of the flow of history in terms of complexity—after all, it is simultaneously impacted by many things: technology, geography, politics, culture, religion, the actions of great men/women, as well as the not-so-great, and sheer luck. Yet, this method of thinking about history is surprisingly recent and is far from universal. History is still largely written as if it is pre-determined by some unidimensional factor: historical materialism, geography, demography, or great men (take your pick). In the case of India, history writing is further complicated by the accumulation of colonial, Nehruvian and Marxist biases that have distorted the narrative to a point of absurdity. Indian history needs to be rewritten but only after the primary evidence has been properly revisited. As and when new evidence arrives, we need to update our views.

The idea of constantly and organically updating one's views/actions through feedback loops shows up in many places in my writings. This derives directly from the view that the real world is fundamentally unstable and unpredictable (i.e., it's not a matter of having a better forecasting model). The best response to such a world, therefore, is to have a good grasp of what is currently happening and to respond quickly and flexibly to the evolving situation. In other words, situation awareness and response matter more than the ability to plan meticulously.

This is not a new idea. The famous nineteenth century Prussian, General Helmut von Molke—who was also a formidable polymath—summed up his theory of military strategy as 'no plan of operations extends with certainty beyond the first encounter with the enemy.' When applied to economics, this approach implies that policymakers should apply themselves to better information-gathering and quick responses, than rely on large-scale plans. In turn, the need for speed and transparency puts a premium on keeping policies simple and flexible. Rigid policies, no matter how detailed, will eventually fail. The same can be said about managing cities. Meticulous urban master plans are no substitutes for active leadership and vision. This is not to suggest that planning is not needed, but its use is to provide the opening gambit and a sense of various options at each stage—forethought rather than foresight.

## INFLUENCES

My worldview derives from many sources ranging from religious philosophy and long-range history, to Chaos Theory and Network Theory—with many of them integrated under a broad CAS framework. Some of the foreign writers and thinkers who have influenced me include Friedrich Hayek, Joseph Schumpeter, Daniel Kahneman, Lee Kuan Yew, Nassim Taleb, Karl Popper, Charles Darwin, Sun Tzu, Vidiadhar Naipaul and Jane Jacobs, to name a few. The Indian influences are even more varied and range from ancient texts such as the Ramayana and Mahabharata, and Kautilya's *Arthashastra* to more modern thinkers such as Swami Vivekananda and Sri Aurobindo. I have also benefitted immensely from the ideas of Vijay Kelkar, Vijay Joshi, Michel Danino and Bibek Debroy.

Nonetheless, the most important source of my thinking perhaps is the *Rig Veda*, arguably the oldest text which is still in use anywhere in the world. The text dating back to the Bronze Age is based on a profound sense of wonder at the universe, and makes the case for the bringing together of diverse ideas and views to understand its meaning. Its easy and organic acceptance of plurality is beautifully expressed in its very last hymn:

*Come together, speak together, let our minds be of one accord,*
*Just like all the ancient gods come together around the sacrificial fire.*
*The place is common, common the assembly, common the mind,*
*So let our varied thoughts come together.*

## THE SELECTION

I had long considered publishing a compendium of my columns and articles, but never really got around to it. So, it was the enthusiasm of my editor, Sudha Sadhanand that really set the ball rolling. Given the diverse subjects, we decided to group the pieces under three categories: History & Culture, Urban Dynamics, and Economics. The pieces are neither selected nor arranged in a chronological order, but are placed to make the overall reading experience more interesting. In the end, the choice of grouping and the order is arbitrary (this is no science, so forgive our idiosyncrasies).

Some of the pieces in this collection required minor editing to remove errors and discrepancies, clarify some terms, and to remove some of the cutesy sub-headings, but the articles have deliberately not been updated. Instead we have added the date of publication, and occasionally also added a few introductory lines, so that the readers get to know the context in which they were written. We felt that the readers may find it more interesting to know what I thought about something at a particular point in time, rather than in hindsight.

# HISTORY & CULTURE

This section deals with a variety of socio-cultural issues ranging from my views on the fundamental nature of Hinduism to the need to re-write Indian history. The reader will instantly recognise the philosophical impact of the complexity theory in many of the articles (indeed, it's explicit in many of them). In most places, I have tried laying out some of the practical implications of my thought processes. This is not to say that I have worked out all the details, but my purpose is to look at the world through a new lens, examine real-world evidence and constantly rework their assumptions about how society functions. I am a fellow-seeker and have no pretentions of being a prophet.

Many of these essays have interesting afterlives. Some of them, particularly those related to history of the Indian Ocean, would later find their way into my book, *The Ocean of Churn*. I am pleased to say that the book (and the articles) have had a discernable impact on how Indians see their place in the Indian Ocean rim and its history. Similarly, my argument that Indian history textbooks need to be revisited is now taken seriously and is no longer seen as a demand from some fringe group (although the actual rewriting has barely begun). The essays about the impending revolt against

India's traditional elite, written in late-2010 early-2011, are now considered common wisdom, but I could have only guessed the political significance of the shift at that time.

This is not to suggest that all my articles were prescient or influential. My suggestions about what should be done to re-ignite Indian languages has not yet, as far as I can tell, had any impact at all. Not that everything in this collection is meant to be taken too seriously. There is a satirical piece on the hotel industry that I hope readers find amusing. We have also included the full version of an interview that I had done with Gayatri Nayak of *The Economic Times*. My editor thought that it may help readers make some sense of me as a person.

# THE ARCHITECTURE OF HINDUISM

S anatan Dharma or Hinduism has long suffered from a very basic problem—the difficulty of defining it. One can describe a particular sect, or philosophy, but it is not easy to explain the whole. Thus, it is not uncommon for people to ultimately fall back on saying that it is a 'way of life'. Unfortunately, such a definition is neither a meaningful description nor of analytical value. If anything, it causes a great deal of confusion by suggesting that Hindu religion is identical to Indic culture—the two are obviously linked, but not exactly the same. The purpose of this piece is to investigate the systemic logic of Sanatan Dharma as a whole and the process by which it evolves. It is not concerned here with the philosophical content or daily practice of any of the constituent sects, traditions and philosophies.

Most world religions, particularly those of Abrahamic origin, are based on a clearly defined set of beliefs—a single god, a holy book, a prophet and so on. These are articles of faith or axioms from which each of these religions is derived. This is why the terms, religion, belief and faith can be used interchangeably in these cases. In contrast, it is perfectly acceptable in Hinduism to be a polytheist, monotheist, monist, pantheist, agnostic, atheist, animist or any combination thereof. Thus Hinduism is a religion but not a faith, although constituent sects or philosophies can be termed faiths or beliefs. Instead, it should be thought of as an organic, evolving ecosystem of interrelated and interdependent elements that are constantly interacting with each other (and with the outside world).

There are many systems that fit the above description—financial markets, economies, cities, the English language, ecological systems and so on. These are all examples of Complex Adaptive Systems or CAS. Note the contrast between the organic and evolving dynamics of such systems and the static laws of Newtonian mechanics. In turn, this has important implications for how we understand Hinduism and manage it.

## NOT THE SUM OF ITS PARTS

One of the most obvious differences between Complex Adaptive Systems and Newtonian mechanical systems is that the former is not the sum of its parts. A mechanical system like a car is the sum total of all its parts as put together to an 'intelligent design'. In contrast, a city is more than the sum of all the buildings; and a biological ecosystem is not just the sum of all the plants and animals. This is why CAS cannot be described from any single perspective. Thus, the English language also cannot be defined through even the most detailed description of its grammar. Similarly, the most detailed description of the Taj Mahal would not define the city of Agra. Yet, speakers of English and the citizens of Agra have little difficultly identifying and using the language and city respectively. The same is true of the Hindus—their so-called difficulty in defining Sanatan Dharma poses no problem in recognising and practicing their religion.

Moreover, the evolving and mutating nature of CAS implies that even the most detailed description is not just insufficient, but fundamentally wrong over time. For instance, given the constant absorption of words and usages in English, an exclusive reliance on Wren & Martin's grammar to understand the language would miss the point. This is also true of Hinduism where even the most detailed reading of the Dharma Shastras and *Smritis* would not give you the correct picture of the lived experience of the religion over time.

## HISTORY DEPENDENT BUT NOT REVERSIBLE

One of the common characteristics of CAS is that they are path-dependent i.e., they carry the imprint of their historical evolution. Thus most cities, biological ecosystems and living languages will show the layer-by-layer accumulation of their history. Readers will no doubt recognise how this applies to Hinduism. Notice how this is distinct from Newtonian mechanics. Two identical footballs, in identical conditions, will behave in exactly the same way if the same force is applied to them. There is no historical memory in the system, and it does not matter what was done with the two balls before we subjected them to this experiment.

Complex Adaptive Systems, however, have an additional property—irreversibility. This means that the system will not reverse to its origin even if all historical events were reversed. Thus, reversing the events of human evolutionary history will not take us back to our ape-like ancestors but to a new species. Similarly, reversing urban history will not take a city back to the original village settlement. It's more likely that one will either be faced with a deserted city like Detroit or a museum city like Venice. Again notice the difference with Newtonian mechanics where a perfect reversal of factors will take the system back exactly to its origin.

An implication of these characteristics is that Hinduism carries its history within, but it cannot return to the 'Golden Age'. It is constantly evolving and moving forward even as it draws inspiration and ideas from its past. The holy books, traditions, customs and tenets of Hinduism should not be seen as a path to an ideal 'Kingdom of God' or the 'Caliphate' to which everyone must revert. Rather, they are the accumulation of knowledge and experience. Critics may argue that the idea of 'Ram Rajya' contradicts this point, but this is a misunderstanding. Many Hindus draw inspiration from the idea of Ram Rajya as a period of prosperity and rule of law, but it is not vision for a return to the Iron Age.

## NO EQUILIBRIUM STATE

Yet another characteristic of Complex Adaptive Systems is that they do not have an equilibrium or steady state in the long run. Again, note the contrast with Newton's laws. However, a corollary is that if the system begins to contract, it can continue with no tendency to self-equilibrate. Thus a city like Detroit kept declining even though conventional theory suggests that falling real estate prices would've attracted back people. Financial markets too behave in this way—it keeps rising past what people think is a 'fair value' and then fall back well below—hardly spending any time at the so-called equilibrium.

This behaviour has important implications on how to manage Complex Adaptive Systems. First, it means that managers should not attempt to hold the system at some preconceived steady state. Rather they need to accommodate the fact that the system is characterised by 'increasing returns to scale' which can spiral the system into expansions or contractions. This does not mean that one should not attempt to manage such ecosystems—far from it, financial markets, cities and even ecological systems can benefit from active management. However, the management should allow for constant movement. A city mayor or a financial market regulator who insists on holding the system to a static equilibrium will either fail or effectively suffocate the system.

Although Hinduism does not have a centralised leadership, the above characteristics have many implications for how Hindus think about their religion and manage its future.

For instance, they suggest that Hindu leaders refrain from being too prescriptive of where Hinduism should go in the long run. It would serve the purpose better if they focus on continuously updating and reforming the system while taking care to maintain internal diversity. The lack of uniformity may seem like a disadvantage in the short-run, but is a big advantage when dealing with an unpredictable long-term future. This is analogous to a species maintaining genetic diversity as a bulwark against epidemics and other shocks.

Another possible implication of this intellectual framework may be that one needs to be less enthusiastic about 'anti-conversion laws'. These have been proposed by some activists as a way to 'protect' Hinduism in some Indian states, but these laws are based on an idea of static equilibrium. Our analysis, however, suggests that such laws will have little benefit if the Hindu community is shrinking for whatever reason. In other words, a defensive tactic cannot work if the community is in a downward spiral in a particular area. It would be far better to focus on expansionary strategies to re-inflate the system. These could include intellectual and cultural innovation, social and missionary work, building alliances with other like-minded religious traditions and so on. Some of these efforts can be derived from the past, but it is perfectly alright to use completely new strategies.

## THE IMPORTANCE OF FLEXIBILITY

One of the learnings from the study of CAS is that in the

long run, flexibility will always triumph over brute strength. Indeed, inflexible systems can sometime disintegrate very suddenly even if they look outwardly strong. Take, for instance, the evolutionary history of life on earth. The dinosaurs were big and strong, and dominated the planet for millions of years. Yet, they suddenly disappeared as they couldn't adapt to changed circumstances—except for a few species who adapted to become birds! Similarly, the erstwhile Soviet Union for all its nuclear warheads, simply collapsed overnight because it could not adapt. China adapted and thrived. A similar story can be told of cities. Once great cities like Birmingham, Detroit and Kolkata were unable to adapt to de-industrialisation. In contrast, by repeatedly reinventing itself, London has not only survived de-industrialisation and the loss of Empire, but able to retain its place as the world's financial capital.

This has very important lessons for Hinduism. Indeed, the religion has survived for so long because it was able to continuously evolve through internal reforms, innovations and absorption. Sometimes it was the slow accumulation of small changes; sometimes it was a rapid shift led by a reformer like Adi Shankaracharya or Swami Vivekananda. There were also many instances where Sanatan Dharma absorbed a foreign idea and made it its own—Hindu temples and idol worship is possibly inspired by the Greeks (Vedic Hindus used only fire altars).

Interestingly, Hinduism's flexible, adaptive architecture may not have appeared entirely by chance, but may have been deliberately set up by ancient rishis. Thus, Hindu scriptures are divided into *Shruti* and *Smriti*. The former are said to have been 'heard' from the gods and are consequently canonical. Strictly speaking, only the first three Vedas— *Rig, Sama, Yajur*—are considered *Shruti* (although many would also include the *Atharva Veda*). All other sacred texts, including the much revered Bhagavad Gita, are considered *Smriti*. The *Smriti* are 'remembered' and therefore considered of human origin—the works of great thinkers, compilations of traditions, and so on. Some of them may be highly regarded, but they are not canonical.

This architecture has had important implications for Hinduism. The *Shruti* texts may be canonical and provide general principles, but they are wonderfully open-ended (just consider the *Nasadiya Sukta* or Creation Hymn in the *Rig Veda* to understand what I mean), whereas the *Smriti* texts are more specific, but not canonical. This means that one can keep adding new texts and ideas forever, including texts that contradict previous *Smriti* texts. The much criticised *Manu Smriti*, by definition, can simply be replaced or revised if Hindus so wish.

To conclude, analysing Hinduism as a Complex Adaptive System provides many important insights into the functional architecture of Sanatan Dharma. It shows that the key strength of Hinduism has been its ability to evolve, adapt and innovate. This potentiality needs to be actively enhanced and strategically deployed in order to keep Hinduism healthy. For instance, it may be time to revive the tradition of writing new *Smriti* texts, a practice that went into decline in the medieval times. Some orthodox Hindus may consider this presumptuous, but as discussed, it would be in keeping with the inherent logic of Sanatan Dharma.

This article merely illustrates some of the possibilities presented by the systemic approach to understanding Hinduism. It is not meant as a comprehensive treatise, but an attempt to initiate a new way of thinking about Sanatan Dharma.

(This piece was originally published in *Swarajya,* November 2014. A version of this article was also published in *Prabodhan,* a collection of essays edited by Dr Saradindu Mukherji, World Hindu Congress, November 2014)

# INDIA MUST START WORKING
# TO REVERSE THE PLUNDER

The organised theft of the country's artistic heritage is perhaps the biggest scandal of modern India and it goes on virtually unnoticed. It is not merely about the sheer scale of plunder, but the erosion of the very soul of our civilisation.

According to experts, around 20,000 idols, sculptures and other antiquities have been stolen and sold in foreign countries since 1980. This excludes colonial-era loot. The estimated market value of these antiquities is over ten billion dollars, although many of these artefacts are priceless from a cultural perspective. Even iconic national monuments such as the Jain temples of Mt Abu have not been spared, many of the idols there being modern replicas.

It is important to note that the systematic plunder of national treasures is not due to petty local thieves, but part of a well-oiled international network run by a handful of criminal organisations. They identify specific pieces, buy off officials to smuggle across borders, use well-known auction houses and even have prominent art experts on their payrolls.

Raids in New York on the warehouses of a single Madison Avenue art dealer Subhash Kapoor unearthed 107 million dollars worth of antiquities, mostly stolen from India. He alone would have channelled billions of dollars worth of artefacts over three decades. There are several such operators in North America, Europe and the Asia-Pacific.

These are not small-scale deals done in shady back alleys. Many of the stolen pieces are proudly displayed in museums and galleries around the world. Meanwhile, the stealing of artefacts, especially temple sculptures, carries on unabated despite the fact that Subhash Kapoor is in jail in Chennai awaiting trial.

The good news is that the authorities have become more aware of the issue. The few high-profile investigations have made museums and private collectors in the West more careful about making purchases. Private citizen initiatives like the India Pride Project have also played an important role in tracking down stolen goods and spreading awareness. This new activism has already led to the recovery of a few idols.

On his state visit to India in September 2015, Australian Prime Minister Tony Abbott handed over an eleventh century Chola Nataraja to Prime Minister. A month later, German Chancellor Angela Merkel handed back a tenth-century idol of Durga stolen from Kashmir two decades ago.

But these are no more than a drop in the bucket. Here are a few simple things that need to be done urgently to turn the tide.

First of all, let us bring back the hundreds of idols and sculptures that have already been identified and seized by law enforcement agencies around the world. The US authorities alone have around 700 pieces stored in their vaults that they can hand over immediately. An additional 1,200 pieces are being processed. There are many artefacts similarly ready for return from Europe. Their return has been reportedly hampered for years because of delays in paperwork on the Indian side. The Indian authorities need to step up their game.

Second, the trade in stolen antiquities is a sophisticated international operation and the local police constable cannot be expected to fight against it effectively. It requires specialist knowledge that can only be expected from a dedicated team.

Italy has had a Carabinieri Art Squad that has so far recovered half a million pieces. It is now training similar teams from Greece, Cambodia and other countries. In India, the only example of a specialist team is Tamil Nadu's Idol Squad, which has had some notable successes despite pitifully limited resources. This needs to be replicated in all states and coordinated at the national level.

Unlike some other branches of criminal investigation, this field can benefit enormously from active participation of scholars, history enthusiasts and temple devotees. Indeed, several successful investigations have depended on critical inputs from private citizens.

Third, a clear framework of property rights needs to be established and enforced to make it possible for enforcement agencies to trace and claim back antiquities. This is essential for countering criminal gangs that have mastered the art of creating a paper trail for their stolen items and even getting well-known scholars to vouch for them.

A National Antiquities Register can be created that allows any owner to register items and makes it easy to look up the ownership history. It should be simple enough to allow me to register my great-grandfather's old watch. The government can easily get this going by recording items from national monuments as well as those from museums. This will have the added benefit of forcing an audit of our museums and archaeology department warehouses.

A lot of work needs to be done to reverse the plunder of our national heritage. However, the above measures would be a good way to start. For once, we are likely to get a lot of international support because the Islamic State (IS) uses the same criminal networks to raise money by selling antiquities from Syria and Iraq. There is not a moment to be lost.

(This piece was originally published in *The Economic Times*, February 2016)

# ASHOKA, THE NOT SO GREAT

Ashoka is commonly eulogised in Indian history textbooks as a great emperor and a pacifist. A current television serial is adding to the legend. The problem is that this is all based on very thin evidence and, even a little bit of probing, suggests a very different story.

In 274 BC, Bindusara suddenly fell ill and died. The crown prince Sushima was away fending off incursions on the north-western frontiers and rushed back to Pataliputra, the royal capital. However, on arrival he found that Ashoka, one of his half-brothers, had taken control of the city with the help of Greek mercenaries. It appears that Ashoka had Sushima killed at the eastern gates. This was followed by four years of a bloody civil war in which Ashoka seems to have killed all male rivals in his family. Buddhist texts mention that he killed ninety-nine half-brothers and only spared his full brother, Tissa. Hundreds of loyal officials were also killed. Having consolidated his power, he was finally crowned emperor in 270 BC.

All accounts agree that Ashoka's early rule was brutal and unpopular, and that he was known as 'Chandashoka' or Ashoka the Cruel. In popular imagination however, Ashoka would invade Kalinga a few years later and, shocked by the death and destruction, would convert to Buddhism and become a pacifist. The reader will be surprised to discover that the narrative about this conversion is almost certainly false. Ashoka would invade Kalinga in 262 BC, whereas we know from minor rock edicts that Ashoka had converted to Buddhism more than two years earlier. Even Ashoka's eulogists like Charles Allen agree that his conversion predated the Kalinga war. Moreover, he seems to have had links with Buddhists for a decade before his conversion. The evidence suggests that his conversion to Buddhism was more to do with the politics of succession than with any regret he felt for the sufferings of war.

The Mauryans most likely followed Vedic court rituals (certainly many of their top officials were Brahmins), but had eclectic religious affiliations in personal life. The founder of the line, Chandragupta seems to have had links to the Jains in his old age, while his son Bindusara seems to have been partial to a heterodox sect called the Ajivikas. This is not an unusual arrangement in the Dharmic family of religions. This eclectic approach remains alive to this day and followers of Dharmic religions think nothing of praying at each other's shrines.

It is likely that when Ashoka usurped the throne, he was opposed by family members who had links with the Jains and the Ajivikas. He may have responded by reaching out to their rivals, the Buddhists, for support. This may explain his later treatment of the Jains and Ajivikas. The power struggle may even explain his invasion of Kalinga. The mainstream view is that Kalinga was an independent kingdom that was invaded by Ashoka, but there is some reason to believe that it was either a rebellious province or a vassal that was no longer trusted.

We know that the Nandas, who preceded the Mauryas, had already conquered Kalinga and, therefore, it is likely that it became part of the Mauryan empire when Chandragupta took over the Nanda kingdom. In any case, it seems odd that a large and expansionist empire like that of the Mauryas would have tolerated an independent state so close to its capital, Pataliputra and its main port at Tamralipti. In other words, Kalinga wouldn't have been an entirely independent kingdom under Bindusara—it was either a province or a close vassal. Something obviously changed during the early years of Ashoka's reign and my guess is that Kalinga had either sided with Ashoka's rivals during the battle for succession and/or declared itself independent in the confusion.

Whatever the real reasons for attracting Ashoka's ire, a large Mauryan army marched into Kalinga around 262 BC. The Kalingans never had a chance. Ashoka's own inscriptions tell us that a lakh died in the war and an even larger number died from wounds and hunger. A further 1,50,000 were taken away as captives.

According to the official narrative, Ashoka was horrified by his own brutality and became a Buddhist and a pacifist. However, as we have seen, he was already a practicing Buddhist when he invaded Kalinga. Moreover, from what we know of his early rule, he was hardly a man to be easily shocked by the sight of blood. The main evidence of his repentance comes from his own inscriptions. However, it is very curious that this 'regret' is mentioned only in locations far away from Odisha (such as in Shahbaz Garhi in north-western Pakistan). None of the inscriptions in Odisha express any remorse; any hint of regret is deliberately left out.

Surely, if Ashoka was genuinely remorseful, he would have bothered to apologise to the people whom he had wronged. Far from it, he does not even offer to free the captives. Even the inscriptions where he expresses regret include a clear threat of violence against other groups like the forest tribes who are unequivocally 'told of the power to punish them that Devanampriya possesses in spite of his repentance, in order that they may be ashamed of their crimes and may not be killed.' This is no pacifist.

It appears that Ashoka was using his inscriptions as a tool of political propaganda to counter his reputation for cruelty. As with the words of any politician, this does not mean he changed his behaviour. Indeed, given that several of his inscriptions are deliberately placed in locations that are difficult to reach, it is quite possible that some of the propaganda was meant for us, rather than his contemporaries. The Sri Lankan text *Ashokavadana* moreover tells us of more acts of genocide perpetrated by the emperor many years after he had supposedly turned pacifist. These were directed particularly at followers of the Jain and Ajivika sects; by all accounts, he avoided conflicts with mainstream Hindus and was respectful towards the Brahmins. The *Ashokavadana* clearly mentions how an enraged Ashoka had 18,000 Ajivikas in Bengal put to death in a single episode. This is the first known instance of large-scale religious persecution in Indian history and sadly, would not be the last.

This is not the only incident mentioned in the text. A Jain devotee was found in Pataliputra drawing a picture showing Buddha bowing to a Jain tirthankara. Ashoka ordered him and his family to be locked inside their home and for the building to be set alight. He then ordered that he would pay a gold coin in exchange for every decapitated head of a Jain. The carnage only ended when someone mistakenly killed his only surviving brother, the Buddhist monk, Vitashoka (also called Tissa). The story points towards frightening parallels with modern-day fundamentalists who kill cartoonists whom they accuse of insulting their religion.

Supporters of Ashoka will claim that these acts of genocide are untrue and that they were inserted into the story by fundamentalist Buddhist writers in later times. This is indeed a possibility, but let me remind readers that my alternative narrative is based on exactly the same texts and inscriptions that are used to praise the emperor. Perhaps the same skepticism should be evenly applied to all the evidence and not just to portions of the text that do not suit the mainstream narrative.

In addition to the evidence of his continued cruelty, we also have proof that he was not a successful administrator. In his later years, an increasingly ailing Ashoka watched his empire disintegrate from rebellion, internal family squabbles, and fiscal stress. While he was still alive, the empire had probably lost some of the north-western territories that had been acquired from Seleucus. Within a few years of Ashoka's death in 232 BC, the Satvahanas had taken over most of the territories in southern India and Kalinga had seceded.

As one can see, Ashoka does not look like such a great king on closer inspection, but as a cruel and unpopular usurper who presided over the disintegration of a large and well-functioning empire. This fits with the fact that he is not remembered as a great monarch in the Indian tradition but in hagiographic Buddhist texts written in countries that did not experience his reign. He was 'rediscovered' in the nineteenth century by colonial era orientalists like James Princep. His elevation to being 'Ashoka the Great' is even more recent and is the result of political developments in the first half of the twentieth century.

When it became clear that it was only a matter of time before India would become free of British rule, some leaders of the freedom movement such as Jawarharlal Nehru decided to create a lineage for their socialist leanings. The problem was that India's ancient political texts did not easily lend itself to this. For instance, the *Arthashastra*, the treatise written by Chandragupta's mentor Chanakya, advocates the main role of the State as ensuring defense, internal security and the rule-of-law; a strong but limited State. It is clearly not a manifesto for the weak but all-pervasive Nehruvian State.

This is when the emerging class of socialist Indian politicians stumbled upon Ashoka's inscriptions. Ashoka clearly spoke of government intervention in the day-to-day lives of his subjects. Indeed, he literally spoke of a nanny State in one of his inscriptions: 'Just as a person feels confident having entrusted his child to an expert nurse thinking "the nurse will keep my child well"; even so the Rajjukas have been appointed by me for the welfare and happiness of the people....'

After Independence, historians were encouraged to further build up the legend of Ashoka the Great in order to provide a lineage to Nehru's socialist project, and the inconvenient evidence about him was simply swept under the carpet. However, a post-socialist reading of Ashoka's inscriptions gives us a very different view of his supposedly welfarist policies. For instance, he created a large cadre of 'dhamma mahammatas' who were supposed to ensure that all subjects adhered to a code of conduct, including several stipulations on what people should eat. We have a modern term for such officials—religious police. It is no surprise that Ashoka's empire collapsed around him.

Writers like Charles Allen patronisingly wrote how ancient Indians were somewhat foolish to have had little regard for a great king like Ashoka. On a closer look, it appears that they knew what they were doing. I'm much more concerned that modern Indians have so easily been taken in by a narrative that is almost certainly false.

(This piece was originally published in *Swarajya*, November 2014. A version of the above text was later published as part of *The Ocean of Churn: How the Indian Ocean Shaped Human History*, Penguin Random House India, 2016)

# THERE'S A DRAGON IN THE SEA

China's growing geostrategic presence in the Indian Ocean is now more than visible: the dual-use port in Gwadar, the naval base in Djibouti, and so on. Interestingly, Chinese empires have tried to assert their influence in the region for over a thousand years. This is a brief history of these early attempts.

At the end of the tenth century, maritime trade boomed between the Song empire in China, the Cholas in India, and the Fatimids in Egypt. There were two main sea routes: through the Strait of Malacca controlled by the Srivijayas of Sumatra/Malaya, and through the Sunda Strait controlled by the Javanese. Not surprisingly, the two were bitter rivals.

In 987 AD, the Srivijayas came under attack from the Javanese and requested the Song emperor for protection. Thus, China came to have influence in the region. The Srivijayas were soon using Chinese backing to expand. Around 1012, the Khmer king Suryavarman I sent an unusual gift to Rajendra Chola: his war-chariot. In the Indic cultural context, such a gift had a great symbolic importance and it appears that the Khmers were trying to woo the Indians to counterbalance the Sino-Sumatran alliance.

In 1016, the Srivijayas defeated the Javanese and ransacked their capital. This left them in control of both the sea routes and the Srivijayas soon began to exploit the situation by exacting exorbitant tolls on merchant ships. The Indians responded. Rajendra Chola probably sent a small naval expedition to Sumatra in 1017 as a warning, but returned in 1025 with a much larger fleet.

The fleet made its way into the Strait of Melaka (Malacca) and systematically ransacked Srivijaya ports. Finally, the Cholas decisively defeated the main army in Kadaram (now the Kedah province in Malaysia), which significantly diminished Srivijayan power.

But remarkably, the Chinese did not do anything in support of their vassals. It is possible that the Chinese were just as annoyed at Srivijayas' rent extraction tactics and had an understanding with the Indians.

The Srivijayas too, seem to have accepted their reduced status. They continued to send ambassadors to the Chola court and participated in a joint diplomatic mission to China. When a Chola naval fleet returned to Kadaram in 1068, it was in support of a Srivijaya king against his local rivals.

The Turkic conquest of India and the Mongol conquest of China and West Asia dissolved the old geopolitical equilibrium in the thirteenth century. In the beginning of the fifteenth century, however, a new Ming emperor decided to fund a series of grand voyages to the Indian Ocean. These were not voyages of exploration, but a display of geopolitical reach.

During 1405–33, the Chinese fleet would make seven voyages to Southeast Asia, India, Sri Lanka, Oman and East Africa. Each voyage included giant 'treasure ships' accompanied by hundreds of smaller vessels and as many as 27,000 men. These voyages were led by the Muslim eunuch admiral, Zheng He.

The first voyage was mostly for information-gathering. After that, the Chinese would use the fleet to push their strategic interests; they backed the Thai against the declining Khmer empire; in India, they probably installed a new Samudrin in Calicut (Kozhikode).

When Zheng visited Sri Lanka during the third voyage, he found the island in a state of civil war. The Chinese captured one of the claimants and took him back to meet the Ming emperor. He was later sent back as part of a plan to ensure Chinese influence over the island. The Chinese would similarly intervene in a war of succession in Sumatra.

Perhaps the one intervention with the most far-reaching historical implication was the support for the new kingdom of Malacca as a counterweight to the Hindu Majapahit of Java.

The founder of Malacca was a prince called Parmeswara. The Chinese would provide him with systematic support and he made at least one trip to China to personally pay obeisance to the Ming emperor.

Interestingly, Malacca was also encouraged to convert to

Islam. Although Zheng was a Muslim, this was primarily viewed as a geostrategic move to create a permanent opposition to the Hindus of Java.

Meanwhile, Malacca prospered under Chinese protection while the Majapahits were steadily pushed back. This was the origin of the steady Islamisation of Southeast Asia. The Javanese princes who refused to convert, eventually withdrew to Bali, where their culture is alive to this day.

Meanwhile, in China, the Confucian mandarins were suspicious of the power accumulated by the eunuchs through their presence in the navy. So, they deliberately undermined the navy. The treasure ships were allowed to rot and the records of the voyages were suppressed.

China would withdraw into centuries of isolationism and leave a vacuum in the Indian Ocean that would be filled by a completely unexpected force: the Portuguese. The Europeans would not only take control of the Indian Ocean, but would soon turn up on China's doorstep.

As one can see, previous Chinese incursions in the Indian Ocean did have major geopolitical consequences. But China itself was unable to benefit from them. While one should not blindly extrapolate history into the future, it is a reminder to today's geostrategic thinkers of the Law of Unintended Consequences.

(This piece was originally published in *The Economic Times*, April 2016)

# KEEPING ALIVE THE SPIRIT
# OF DURGA PUJA

For much of eastern India, particularly Bengal, Durga Puja is the single most important annual festival. The city of Kolkata bursts into celebrations that rival the carnival in Rio in terms of the sheer scale of cultural outpouring. The extraordinary artistic creativity on display is awe-inspiring and its egalitarian openness to all people, including non-believers, is admirable. Moreover, the popularity of the festival has steadily spread over the last several decades. It was driven initially by the enthusiasm of Bengali communities living in other parts of India and the world, but now one finds it independently celebrated by Hindus who may have nothing to do with its origins in eastern India.

All of this is a good thing. However, there may be a reason to pause for a moment and reflect on the danger that something of the original spirit of Durga Puja may be lost in the increasingly elaborate celebrations and the growing commercialised/professionalised approach towards managing events.

Firstly, in the race to display ever more artistic creativity and grander spectacles, the original simplicity of the religious tradition is eroding. The tradition is clear that the idol must be made of unbaked clay that is meant to dissolve without trace when immersed in a river or other water-body. Unfortunately, as the idols have become more elaborate, artisans have begun to use paints, plaster and other materials that do not entirely disappear without trace. Add to this, the material which is used for building 'pandals', that make a statement. This goes against the very idea of the goddess merging back with the elements of the universe at the end of the festivities.

Secondly, with the emphasis on artistic wizardry, something of the sacred is being lost. Durga Puja holds a deep spiritual significance to the millions who follow the Shakta stream within Hinduism. The morning 'anjali', the evening 'arati', the 'Chandi path', the 'dhunichi' dance to the beating of 'dhak' drums are all central to the festival. The shift to grand spectacles and large crowds can distract from the personal link that devotees feel for the Mother Goddess. It is important that we do not undermine the sanctity of the festival.

Third, a key part of Durga Puja is the way in which it brings together the community. It is about the shared meals served by members of the community to each other. It is about amateur cultural performances in the evening by boys and girls, even adults, of the neighbourhood. Admittedly some of the amateur performances can be awful, but it does not matter—the cycle of practice sessions and preparations are an important part of the shared memories of Durga Puja and anchors many a lasting friendships. By turning over the communal meal to caterers and the cultural performances to professional artists, something of the community spirit is lost.

I am aware that I may be sounding like an old uncle hankering after the good old days. Let me be clear that I am not against innovation and creativity—and am very much in favour of the artistic energy on display. I also know that the festival generates income for thousands of artisans, caterers and other service providers. However, it is important not to lose sight of the actual purpose of the festival and ensure that the original spirit of the tradition is not lost: community participation cannot be replaced by event managers; amateur performances cannot all be replaced by professional artists; and mindless spectacle cannot replace the sacred nature of the festival. Of course, all living traditions must change with the times, but the purpose of innovation must be to bolster the tradition and not dilute it.

(This piece was originally published in *Swarajya*, October 2015)

# INVESTING IN THE LONG-TERM FUTURE OF HINDUISM

All religions have a keen sense of their past. Not surprisingly, this is also true of Hinduism/Sanatan Dharma, the world's oldest religion. Hence a lot of discussion among practicing Hindus focuses on ancient texts, rituals, places of worship and so on. This is natural and healthy as it links the Hindu to the thoughts, ideas and traditions passed down from those who came before them. However, Hinduism is an evolving religion and is wired to constantly update itself while maintaining an umbilical cord to the past—*continuity with change*. Much has been written in recent years about the issue of continuity, but there is perhaps not enough debate on the issue of change. Therefore, the time has come to also look forward and anticipate the issues that will be important to the Hindu community in the twenty-first century.

## THE PROBLEM OF NEXT GENERATION PRIESTHOOD

For millennia, Hinduism has depended to a large extent, albeit not exclusively, on hereditary priesthood from the Brahmin community. Hindu communities that use non-Brahmin priests are also often hereditary in nature. This has allowed rituals, texts and traditions to be passed on from generation to generation even in the face of invasions, persecution and other forms of disruption. However, modernity now presents a very different problem—most of the children of today's priests no longer want to carry on with the family profession. This is partly due to the wide array of economic opportunities available to educated youth outside of priesthood, and partly due to the fact that it no longer enjoys the same prestige.

Some of the next generation may continue to learn certain texts and rituals out of personal interest, but the wider community will no longer be served by such a priesthood. This is likely to become a very serious issue within a generation. Indeed, I have seen many parts of India where the migration of Brahmin youth to cities has left villages without any priests and the village temple is left virtually abandoned.

The central problem is that the Hindu priesthood is very poorly paid. A tiny number of important temples may be able to pay their priests reasonable salaries, but for the most part, they are very poorly paid. Even in the case of a major temple, the salaries can be abysmal. For instance, the head priest of Rajagopalaswamy Kulasekhara Azhwar temple in Tamil Nadu earns a mere Rs 750 per month.[1] This is absurd for a profession that needs dedication and knowledge. Most priests make a living by officiating at occasional ceremonies or running small temples where incomes are even more erratic. As a result, a large proportion of the priesthood has been reduced to a state of extreme penury, no better than beggars. Hindu priests have faced poverty in the past, but they held a position of prestige in the community when economic alternatives were limited. This has now changed.

The obvious first order solution is to encourage non-Brahmin men and women to enter priesthood and run important religious institutions. Indeed, we see some of this happening organically. For instance, Kanhaiya Shivanand Giri, a Dalit, was recently made the Mahamandaleshar of Juna Akhara. While this may provide some intake, my sense is that the economic considerations that influence Brahmin youth will also impact non-Brahmins. So, one may get a few committed individuals, but not enough to make up for the rapid depletion in hereditary priesthood. Indeed, Hindu communities that traditionally use non-Brahmin priests will also face exactly the same problem soon.

This short essay does not pretend to have found an answer. The purpose here is to merely flag a very important issue that is simply not getting adequate attention from the wider community. A full range of solutions will be needed ranging from institutionalising a system of part-time priests

---

1  http://www.thehindu.com/society/faith/petition-on-temple-priests-salary/article23443980.ece

to increasing salaries at least in those temples where resources are available. Hindu communities living outside India have found creative solutions to this problem, particularly in the US, and these should be explored.

## UPDATING OF RITUALS AND TRAINING OF PRIESTS

Sanatan Dharma is an evolving religion and its strength lies in its ability to keep changing and absorbing new ideas. For instance, Vedic Hindus did not worship idols or build temples, but these are now intrinsic parts of the religion. We now need to think actively about how to adapt Hinduism for the twenty-first century while maintaining its links to the past. One thing that needs attention is the updating of common rituals.

All religions require common rituals that bring a sense of continuity and community. Unfortunately, the term 'ritualism' often has a negative connotation. The problem is that many Hindu rituals are seen even by ardent adherents as being outdated. There are many reasons for this—the rituals no longer carry the same symbolic meanings; they may be too expensive to perform or time-consuming; Hindus living outside India find it especially difficult to keep up with many practices. All this requires rethinking of rituals.

Of course, Hinduism does not have a centralised church that can carry out the changes. It will eventually have to be an organic, democratic process. However, concerned Hindus need to apply their mind to this issue, and to the problem of training priests in the new system. Note that this must be done carefully and with a light touch so that it does not impact continuity or plurality of little traditions.

## NEED TO PROTECT THE 'LITTLE TRADITIONS'

Hinduism is made up of a multitude of traditions, great and small. In addition to the major texts and mainstream temples/festivals, Hinduism is a bubbling ecosystem of local deities, village shrines, tribal customs and family traditions. Unfortunately, modernity and migration is causing many of these local forms of Hinduism to be lost. Some Hindus may take the view that there is no need to bemoan the disappearance of such diversity. In fact, a few may argue that the resultant homogeneity is a good thing and may strengthen Hinduism, but I disagree.

From the very beginning, Hinduism has consciously tried to provide space for different forms of religious expression. The last hymn of the *Rig Veda*, the oldest and most sacred Hindu text, explicitly states:

> *Come together, speak together, let our minds be of one accord,*
> *Just like all the ancient gods come together around the sacrificial fire.*
> *The place is common, common the assembly, common the mind,*
> *So let our varied thoughts come together.*

Quite apart from maintaining the inherent plurality of

Hinduism, these 'little traditions' are very important to keep it alive as a whole because they provide 'genetic diversity'. The incredible longevity of Sanatan Dharma owes a lot to this, because genetic diversity provides a large pool of ideas that can be used to survive changing circumstances. For instance, Ganesh Chaturthi was a little tradition in Maharashtra that was leveraged up by Tilak a hundred years ago as part of political mobilisation against British rule. Today, it is not only a major mainstream festival in Maharashtra, but has spread to all parts of the country.

To be fair, it may not be practical to save every little tradition and custom. Indeed, many such traditions appeared and vanished in the course of Sanatan Dharma's long history. This is part of the natural evolution of the religion. Nonetheless, a conscious effort needs to be made to maintain some of the diversity that defines Hinduism while allowing for organic evolution at the same time. At the very least, an effort needs to be made to record them for posterity in texts, photographs and videos.

## WHY HINDUISM SHOULD BE A MISSIONARY RELIGION

There is a general perception that Hinduism has never been a missionary religion. Individual sects may take up missionary work, but Hinduism as a whole is seen as inherently incapable of proselytising. However, this flies against a pile of historical evidence that Hinduism was widely practiced outside the Indian subcontinent in ancient and medieval times from Central Asia to South East Asia. The largest Hindu temple ever built is not in India but in Cambodia. This spread of Hinduism took place peacefully through commercial and cultural exchange—but also involved active efforts to spread Dharmic ideas. Sadly, this spirit withered away in the thirteenth century as Hindus turned inward and imposed rules on themselves against crossing the seas.

Today, some sects and spiritual gurus have taken to actively spreading their ideas both within and outside India. One may ask why Hinduism as a whole should undertake this task rather than leave it to these separate groups. In my view, Hinduism is a framework that allows for the co-existence of an extraordinary variety of ideas, beliefs and ways of life. No constituent belief or sect can substitute for the overall framework. After a lapse of many centuries, we live in a time when people worldwide are losing faith in unidimensional religions and prescriptive ideologies. Thus, the moment has come to spread a framework that consciously allows for plurality.

(This piece was originally published in *Prabodhan II: Some Thoughts on Hindu Society*, edited by Dr Saradindu Mukherji, World Hindu Congress, 2018)

# GREAT MEN DO MAKE HISTORY

The news of Nelson Mandela's death brings back personal memories of a time when South Africa could have gone in many directions. The South Africa we see today owes much to the philosophical evolution and personal example of one man. It would have taken very little for the country to have turned out as another Zimbabwe or even another Somalia.

My first visit to South Africa was in the tumultuous summer of 1993. I was then a student at Oxford University and had somehow managed to get myself funded to work on a development project in a remote tribal 'homeland' for two and a half months. My passport still read, 'Not valid for the Republic of South Africa', although the Indian government had removed restrictions just a few weeks earlier. My visa was not stamped on the passport, but was given on a separate sheet of paper.

The South Africa I visited was still heavy with the reminder of the apartheid era. Racial segregation had been abolished only a few months earlier, but public toilets still read 'White' and 'Coloured'. Nelson Mandela had been freed, but the white-run government was still in place. I lived and worked in the tribal homeland of KaNgwane along the Swaziland border—one of the many 'nominally autonomous reservations' created for the black population (it is now part of the province of Mpumalanga). However, even in the remote savannah grassland and hills of the Low Veldt, there was palpable tension in the air.

To the outside world, South Africa's internal tensions appeared as black versus white. However, the situation on the ground was much more complicated. The white population was split between those who favoured the changes, and those who clung on to the hope of some form of return to segregation. There were also the age-old suspicions between English-speaking whites of British origin and Afrikaans-speaking whites of Dutch origin. The wounds of the Boer wars of 1880–1881 and 1899–1902 still hadn't been completely healed.

The black population was similarly divided on tribal lines. The Zulu nationalist Inkatha Freedom Party was suspicious of the African National Congress or ANC (Nelson Mandela and many ANC leaders belonged to the rival Xhosa tribe). As the apartheid regime crumbled, these rivalries increasingly spiralled into bloodshed. In just one of the incidents, dubbed the Boipatong massacre, forty people were killed and many more were injured. By the summer of 1993, all sides were stockpiling arms. My camp was on the route used to smuggle arms from nearby Mozambique and on one occasion my pickup truck (locally called a 'bakkie') was hijacked at gunpoint. Luckily, I was not driving it at that time, but my co-worker had to walk many miles back to the camp. The vehicle was found abandoned a few days later.

As if this was not complicated enough, there were other groups including Indians and those of mixed race. The latter formed a large segment of the population in the western half of the country, but found themselves stuck in a cultural and political no-man's land. The Indian population was scattered, but it had a significant concentration around the eastern city of Durban (Mahatma Gandhi had been thrown out of the train in nearby Pietermaritzburg). Although it had faced discrimination under apartheid, the industrious community had come to control much of the country's retail and wholesale trade and become fairly prosperous. Not surprisingly, all other groups resented them. In fact, as I found out, virtually every group suspected that the Indians were funding their rivals!

Over that summer, I witnessed riots at Witwatersrand University in Johannesburg, attended political rallies in seething townships, and listened to the regular hum of distant gunfire. A white-supremacist group even managed briefly to take over the World Trade Centre, Kempton Park, where multi-party negotiations were taking place. South Africa was a country on the boil and I met many white families who were making plans of leaving the country and moving to the United States, Britain or Australia.

As I think about that period, it becomes clear how easily the country could have gone into a spiral of violence and retribution. It is to Nelson Mandela's extraordinary achievement that he was able to somehow reconcile the country's many internal contradictions and carry people along with him. Equally commendable is the fact that, unlike many leaders of newly-freed countries, he did not yield to the temptation of holding on to power till his death or of perpetuating a dynasty. Modern historians tend to be dismissive of the 'Great Man Theory' of history and argue that it is history that creates great men—but I think an exception should be made for Mandela.

(This piece was originally published in *Business Standard*, December 2013)

# INDIAN LANGUAGES FACE A THREAT OF FOSSILISATION, NEED REVITALISATION

India has now been a free country for seventy-odd years. Over these decades, we have made progress in many spheres of activity, but there is one area where things seem to be sharply deteriorating—the state of Indian languages. I am not merely referring to the 220-odd minor languages and dialects than we have lost since the 1960s, but the condition of major languages with tens of millions of speakers. This is hardly the first time someone has raised the issue, but the usual thinking is that Indian languages are being hurt by mutual suspicion combined with the apathy of an English-speaking elite. However, there may now be an even bigger threat—fossilisation.

Harivansh Rai Bachchan is one of the most important figures in Hindi literature, but his great grand-children are almost certainly more comfortable in English than in Hindi. This is neither a unique situation nor can it be blamed solely on lingering colonial attitudes in elite schools. Across the country, this is being experienced by otherwise rooted families who are proud of their linguistic heritage.

The professional usefulness of English too is not a credible explanation. Indians have long been comfortable with a link language that was different from what they used in their daily lives. Over centuries, Sanskrit, Persian and English were used for official, commercial, and legal documents, as well as high culture and so on. Far from displacing local languages, they enriched them with new words, ideas and themes. This is why the greatest writers and poets in most Indian languages were often multilingual and happily borrowed from link languages.

In my view, the current crisis in Indian languages comes from a set of interlinked factors that are holding them back from evolving with the times. The first problem is that school textbooks are hopelessly outdated. I have personally verified this for Bengali and Hindi, but also asked parents of children learning other languages.

In lower grades, textbooks typically have a smattering of folktales, stories from the *Panchatantra* and the epics, the lives of folk heroes and so on. These are acceptable as they are timeless; analogous to nursery rhymes and fairy tales in English. However, the rest of the material seems stuck somewhere between the 1930s and 1970s. A survey of the technology reflected in the stories is quite telling. Forget mobile phones and laptops, you will rarely find television sets or even an aircraft. It is still a world of steam engines and animal husbandry.

Matters do not improve in higher grades—a great deal of preaching about 'good habits' and the need to help the poor. These may be worthy goals, but why do Indian language classes need to be specifically burdened with them? There is simply no sense of fun in the material. This is no way to promote a language in a country where the young, including the poor, are so aspirational. Munshi Premchand's *Idgah* may be a great story but, at the risk of offending his fans, it may no longer resonate with most school children.

The second major problem with Indian languages is that the output of innovative new literature has slowed down drastically. Allowing for the odd exception, publishing is increasingly limited to literary novels aimed at winning government awards rather than engaging readers. Once there was a flourishing culture of writing science fiction, detective novels and travelogues in languages like Bengali, but these have slowed to a trickle.

Less than a decade ago, pretentious literary writing was strangling English publishing till the arrival of Chetan Bhagat, Amish Tripathi and Devdutt Pattanaik. Whatever one thinks of their writing styles, there is no denying that they opened up the field. A similar revolution in popular writing needs to happen in other languages. The steadily improving editorial quality of Indian language newspapers shows that there is demand for good writing.

The third related problem is a dearth of translations into Indian languages. A Tamil or Marathi writer will be pleased that his/her novel has been translated into a foreign language. While this may be good for the personal reputation of the writer, it does little for Tamil or Marathi. A language is a medium for transmitting ideas and its repertoire grows as it absorbs material from elsewhere. The success of English lies in the fact that we can read Homer and Kapuscinski without having to learn ancient Greek or Polish. Therefore, inward translation is more important than outward translation. For several languages, translation is an area where government support may be critical to creating a minimum ecosystem of material.

Popular culture depicted in cinema and television are today the most important factors that have kept Indian languages alive. However, these will not be enough in the long run if they do not keep evolving by generating and absorbing new material that fires the imagination of successive generations.

(This piece was originally published in *Hindustan Times*, October 2016)

# LIP SERVICE ONLY

The reality of twenty-first century life is that many of us are forced to travel frequently on business. This is likely to be true whether you are a software engineer, journalist, banker, airline pilot, sports star, Bollywood actor or a professor. Sometimes it is fun, but often it is mundane and tiring: the jetlag, the long wait in the airport lounge, the search for taxis in an unfamiliar and wet city, the expensive but uniformly tasteless food. The hotel is then supposed to be a refuge, a home away from home.

Yet, it is extraordinary that the vast and lucrative hotel industry is so completely insensitive to the needs of the average business traveller. Having endured outrage after outrage, I have decided to raise a flag of revolt against this unbearable tyranny. I hope that this article will instigate a general uprising from my fellow travellers and force change—yes, we can!

The hotel industry likes to say that it pays great attention to the little things that make a guest comfortable. When pressed for specific examples, hotel managers will inevitably fall back on that irritating orchid that they place every night on the bed. However, I have never met anyone to whom it makes the slightest difference. Most will just flick the flower off the sheets and never give it a thought. Personally, I would rather lower my carbon footprint by not importing orchids from halfway around the world.

Let us then turn to matters that really matter. Take, for instance, the 'Master Switch' that hotels place next to the bed. The idea presumably is that you get into bed, read for a few minutes, switch off all the lights with a single flick and then roll over to sleep.

This never happens in reality for there is always a lamp on the other side of the room that is inexplicably not connected to the Master Switch. The tired traveller must then kick off the blanket and trudge across to the lamp only to discover that there is no obvious way to turn it off. In the end, the only solution, short of calling the emergency hotline, is to crawl under the table and pull out the plug. By this time, the poor hotel guest is wide awake and unable to fall asleep.

I would have accepted the failures of the Master Switch as mere negligence, but I have growing evidence of deliberate malice. I once stayed at a well-known hotel in London that had been recently refurbished to look 'cool' by one of those celebrity designers. As a seasoned road warrior, I cleverly switched off the lights before getting into bed as I fully expected to have to deal with that irritating lamp. This time the lamps went off, but the frame of the television lit up in a bright, neon blue. After struggling for fifteen minutes to turn off this eerie apparition, I gave up and called the reception for help. The duty manager told me that the light could not be switched off without turning off the electricity supply of the whole floor! He then haughtily informed me that this was the brilliant idea of some famous designer. Ultimately, the only way I could fall asleep was to place a pillow on top of my face to block out the glow of fluorescent blue.

There are many more examples of such premeditated persecution. The most damning evidence comes from the way hotel showers are designed. It usually requires a doctorate in quantum physics to work out how to get the water to the correct temperature. The more expensive the hotel, the more likely you are to be faced with a bewildering array of knobs and buttons of no known function. As with Heisenberg's Uncertainty Principle, one can never know which direction is hot and which cold. How much would it cost to mark them blue and red? Or, as I suspect, it is deliberate malice.

I can see the hotel staff rolling with laughter at the annual staff party as they imagine their guests being alternately frozen and scalded in the shower.

One cannot even be sure if one will get a dry towel when one is finished with the harrowing bathing experience. Many hotels like to place the bath towels in a place they are guaranteed to get wet as soon as the shower is turned on. On a recent visit to a hotel in Jakarta, I found the stack of towels arranged on a wooden stool placed directly under the shower. A purple orchid had been artistically placed on top as if it would somehow block off the deluge. Who thought of that? Does the orchid have the same significance as the mocking signs that serial killers leave behind at the crime scene?

All this raises some issues of international importance. Are the similarities in these experiences around the world a mere coincidence or is the global hotel industry secretly coordinating its terrorist activities? Is there a school where new recruits are taught that room service always takes 'at least forty minutes' irrespective of what has been ordered? The community of business travellers need to wake up to the danger before it is too late.

(This piece was originally published in *Business Standard*, August 2012)

# HISTORY OF INDIAN OCEAN SHOWS HOW OLD RIVALRIES CAN TRIGGER RISE OF NEW FORCES

After hundreds of years of dominating the Indian Ocean and the broader region, the West is gradually withdrawing. This is allowing the emergence of new geopolitical dynamics. In the Middle East, we see a Sunni alliance led by Saudi Arabia, and Turkey pitted against a Shia alliance led by Iran. Meanwhile, China is establishing its footprint in the region with bases in Djibouti and Gwadar, Pakistan. It is simultaneously expanding into Southeast Asia with claims over the Spratly Islands.

Interestingly, both sets of developments echo geopolitical dynamics that played themselves out in the Indian Ocean rim before the arrival of the Europeans. Revisiting this history provides interesting insights into the long-term implications of such rivalries.

## ....NTINES VERSUS PERSIANS

In the sixth century AD, the Middle East was dominated by two powers—a Christian alliance led by the Byzantine empire and the Sasanian empire of Iran. The main regional ally of the Byzantines was Ethiopia that had recently converted to orthodox Christianity. One of the factors that drove the rivalry was control over the Yemen-Oman coast as it was key to trade with India. As a contemporary Byzantine put it, 'For it is impossible for the Ethiopians to buy cloth from the Indians, since the Persian merchants always locate themselves in the very harbours where the Indians first put in.'

The Ethiopian king Ella Asbeha tried several times to place a Christian on the Yemeni throne. However, each time the Ethiopian army withdrew, the Jewish and pro-Persian factions rose in revolt. Finally, Ella Asbeha left behind a large Ethiopian garrison, but the soldiers went rogue and placed their own candidate on the throne. This was the way in which Yemen was devastated by a complicated civil war. Eventually, the Persians intervened and took over the coast.

As if the Byzantine–Persian wars were not bad enough, the region suffered a deadly pandemic. Known as the Plague of Justinian, it spread across the Mediterranean and the Middle East killing an estimated twenty-five to fifty million people. Thus, when the seventh century dawned, the northwestern rim of the Indian Ocean was exhausted from war and disease. When the Arabs suddenly rose under the banner of Islam, the Byzantines and the Persians were simply too depleted to respond.

The Yemeni and Omani tribes fighting Persian rule were among the earliest groups to convert to Islam. The Arabs next defeated the Sasanians at the Battle of Qadisiyyah in 637 AD and took over their empire. The last embers of Sasanian culture now survive as the tiny Parsi community in India. The Byzantines were similarly forced back into their heartlands in Anatolia (what is now Turkey). Their empire would slowly shrink to a small area around their capital Constantinople till Ottoman Turks captured and renamed it Istanbul.

## THE CHINESE TREASURE FLEET

At the beginning of the fifteenth century, the Ming emperor of China decided to fund a series of grand voyages to the Indian Ocean. Note that these were not voyages of exploration as the routes had been well-known for hundreds of years. Instead, it was a display of geopolitical reach. Remember that the Chinese had only recently overthrown the Mongols and were keen to establish their position in the world; much like today's China.

Between 1405 and 1433, the Chinese fleet would make seven voyages to Southeast Asia, India, Sri Lanka, Oman and East Africa. The fleets included giant 'treasure ships' accompanied by hundreds of smaller vessels and as many as 28,000 men. The unlikeliest of people led the expeditions—a Muslim eunuch called Zheng He from landlocked Yunnan (see, chapter titled, There's a Dragon in the Sea, p. 25).

The Chinese would soon use the fleet to re-arrange the

geopolitical landscape of the Indian Ocean. They backed the Thais against the Khmers. In India, they seem to have installed a new Samudrin in Kozhikode. They found Sri Lanka in a state of civil war, so one of the claimants to the throne was captured and taken to meet the Ming emperor. He was later sent back as part of a plan to ensure Chinese influence over the island. Zheng He similarly intervened in a war of succession in Sumatra.

Perhaps the most significant intervention was support for the new kingdom of Malacca as a counter-weight to the Majapahit of Java. The Hindu Majapahit were the most powerful maritime power in the Indian Ocean at that time and were opposed to Chinese intrusion into their sphere of influence.

Meanwhile, the Chinese provided systematic support to Malacca and its king made at least one trip to personally pay obeisance to the Ming emperor. Interestingly, the kingdom was also encouraged to convert to Islam to create a permanent opposition to the Hindus of Java. Malacca prospered under Chinese protection while the Majapahit were steadily pushed back. Eventually the Javanese princes who refused to convert, withdrew to Bali where their culture is alive to this day.

Back in China, however, the Confucian mandarins were suspicious of power accumulated by the eunuchs through the navy, and therefore deliberately undermined the navy. The treasure ships were allowed to rot and the records of the voyages were suppressed. China withdrew into centuries of isolationism and left a vacuum in the Indian

Ocean that would be filled by an unexpected entrant—the Portuguese.

An important lesson of history is that geopolitical rivalries often have unintended consequences and can trigger the rise of a completely new force. The incessant Byzantine-Sasanian wars created the conditions that led to the expansion of Arabs. The Chinese fleet cleared the Indian Ocean of local powers but, by withdrawing suddenly, it left a vacuum that was filled by the Europeans. This would eventually lead to the humiliation China suffered at the hands of colonial powers. Of course, history does not repeat itself exactly but, as Mark Twain put it, it often rhymes.

(This piece was originally published in *The Times of India,* August 2016)

# OUR HISTORY BOOKS NEED REWRITING

The debate over the need to re-write Indian history textbooks is heating up and, yet again, it is likely to spiral into an ugly political spat. Sadly this debate will distract from the many sensible reasons history books need to be changed.

Indian history is mostly written from the perspective of Delhi or at most northern India, as if the rest of the country barely existed except as mere provinces. The average Indian student, for instance, will learn almost nothing about the great Satavahana, Vijayanagar or Chola empires of southern India. Unless you live in the northeast, you may never have heard of the Ahom kings who ruled Assam for 600 years and even defeated the Mughals. This absurd imbalance needs to be corrected. Moreover, history is not just about the rise and fall of empires, but also about other streams of history. For instance, Indian textbooks say almost nothing about the country's rich maritime history beyond a passing reference to Chola naval raids on Southeast Asia. Students learn very little about the thriving Indo–Roman trade or the exploits of ancient Odiya merchants who pioneered sea routes across eastern Indian Ocean. The great influence of Indian civilisation on Southeast Asia is barely mentioned, if at all.

We hear about groups who came to India as conquerors but nothing of people who came to India peacefully as traders and refugees—Parsis and Jews from the West, and the waves of Southeast Asian tribes from the east. Similarly, even university-level textbooks are written as if the geographical landscape of the country is static. Little is mentioned of shifting coastlines and rivers, changing wildlife, and evolving cities.

The extraordinary history of Indian science is similarly ignored or, as some would argue, deliberately downplayed. There is more than adequate evidence that ancient Indians made great advances in metallurgy, medicine, mathematics and so on. As others have also pointed out, by downplaying genuine scientific contributions, textbook writers have created a vacuum that is filled with claims of flying chariots.

Most readers will be surprised to know that many well-known events and characters of Indian history are based on very thin evidence. Emperor Ashoka is much revered for having turned into a pacifist after witnessing the human cost of his invasion of Kalinga (see, chapter titled, Ashoka, The Not So Great, p. 18). However, texts such as *Ashokavadana* clearly mention major massacres of Jains and Ajivikas that he ordered long after his supposed conversion. Far from being Ashoka the Great, the evidence suggests an unpopular king whose empire began to crumble while he was still alive. Even the regret over the Kalinga war looks suspiciously like propaganda given that none of the inscriptions in Odisha mention it.

Not only have mainstream historians built grand stories on wobbly evidence, they are also strangely impervious to the continuous flow of new evidence being thrown up by archaeology, genetics, climate sciences and so on. Thus, we are still taught about the Aryan invasion in 1500 BC that destroyed Harappan cities despite the fact that genetic and archeological studies do not support a unidirectional migration/invasion from Central Asia. The date of 1500 BC was always arbitrary and we have good reason to believe that climate change caused the decline of Harappan cities five centuries earlier.

This is not to suggest that everything good about Indic civilisation is of indigenous origin. Over the centuries, we gained from absorbing foreign ideas and influences, especially in food, architecture, and language. Try to imagine India without the chillies and tomatoes brought by the Portuguese, cricket and railways brought by the British, or the Taj Mahal built by a Turko-Mongol emperor. However, it is also true that the same foreign invaders caused the death of millions of people through warfare and famine. Indian students need to be told about both the good and the bad.

Readers will be amazed by the extent to which colonial era ideas are casually perpetuated. For instance, whenever I write an article mentioning ancient Indians, I have noticed that a sub editor will often put the word "Indian" in inverted commas. It is probably done unconsciously, but it is a continuation of colonial-era propaganda that Indians were not a nation till the British turned up. For obvious reasons, colonial writers blatantly disregarded heaps of evidence that Indians had a strong sense of belonging to a civilisation for thousands of years. What is less obvious is why we continue to perpetuate the colonial-era idea.

Indian history textbooks need to be rewritten. Opponents will argue that the current government will use this opportunity to insert 'Right-wing biases', but this is no excuse for perpetuating outdated scholarship and the biases of colonial and Marxist historians. Indian historians tend to mix up the evidence with their opinions. This happens everywhere to some extent as all history is written from some perspective, but mainstream Indian historians are notorious for doing so.

Perhaps one way forward for the next generation of textbook authors is to separate the hard evidence from their interpretations. This will result in two good outcomes. First, it will make the author's opinions more transparent. Second, it will encourage students to think more critically and draw their own conclusions.

Additionally, this will have the advantage of making the subject more an exploration of the past rather than memorising dates.

(This piece was originally published in *Mint*, June 2015)

# WHY RETRIEVED ANTIQUITIES SHOULD BE SENT BACK TO PLACE OF ORIGIN

The industrial scale plunder of Indian antiquities over the three decades is shocking to say the least. Since 1980, around 20,000 idols, sculptures and other antiquities have been stolen and sold in foreign countries. Their market value is estimated at ten billion dollars, although in cultural terms, many of the pieces are priceless. This excludes items looted during the colonial era and in the decades immediately after Independence.

It is important to recognise that the systematic plunder of our antiquities is not the work of small-time thieves acting independently but part of a sophisticated international mafia that includes criminal gangs, corrupt government officials, well-known art experts, and auction houses. These are often the same global networks used in recent years by the Islamic State (IS) to sell artifacts stolen from sites in Syria and Iraq.

One may notice how items are systematically identified and targeted. They were often taken from iconic, protected monuments such as the Jain temples of Mount Abu, and visitors will be shocked to know that they are frequently shown modern replicas.

Unfortunately, there was almost no effort till recently to stop the plunder. Not a single artefact was brought back between 2000 and 2012. The situation has since improved a little with the Indian police, particularly after Tamil Nadu's Idol Wing, arresting a few kingpins. The role of the trade in funding the IS has made foreign governments more vigilant. Authorities have also been helped by a network of art history enthusiasts led by Singapore-based Vijay Kumar who tracked down several pieces in galleries and museums around the world.

As a result, around twenty pieces have been retrieved from abroad in the last two years. Another 2,900 seized items are currently lying with the United States' authorities alone. Hundreds more have been identified in Switzerland and Britain. However, this is barely a drop in the ocean and the flow of stolen items, on balance, is still outward. Repatriation is often hampered by the slow pace at which paperwork is processed by the Indian bureaucracy.

Even as criminal investigations are expanded, there is a growing debate about what the authorities should do with the antiquities that have been retrieved? For some, it is obvious that the pieces should be given back to the individuals or institutions from whom they were stolen. However, there are others who feel that the pieces should be kept under the custody of the government and the best pieces should be displayed in museums.

Having considered the matter from different angles, I have concluded that the artifacts should be sent back to their place of origin unless there is an overriding reason for not doing so. First of all, there is a simple principle that applies to all stolen goods. Whether it is a car or a piece of jewellery, the first claim remains with the original owner. No one else, including the government, has a natural claim. This should apply to antiquities as well. Expropriation by the State is not justice.

Second, it is not obvious that the government will prove to be a more responsible custodian. Indeed, many pieces have been stolen from archaeological sites, monuments, and other sites managed by the government. For instance, crores of rupees worth of Vakataka-era coins were stolen from Nagpur University. Even the report on the theft went missing till it was finally traced in April this year. Indeed, it has been alleged that the slow pace of repatriation paperwork is partly due to the fact that government agencies do not want to acknowledge that certain pieces were stolen from under their noses.

Third, the experience is that retrieved antiquities are rarely displayed and end up in a warehouse. Indian museums are in a poor state and unable to exhibit even their existing collections. The famous Pathur Nataraja, for instance, was retrieved from Britain in 1991 but has not been seen since. Such an approach serves no purpose. Art history lovers have no access to the artifacts even as there is a continued risk that the pieces will be stolen again and/ or replaced with replicas.

Finally, one needs to recognise that many of the items, particularly the temple idols, are part of a living tradition. Their creators did not see them as isolated pieces of art but as part of a broader cultural ecosystem. This is different from how we treat ancient Greek or Roman statues that were part of a dead culture. In contrast, returning temple idols to their place of origin is important for preserving the associated culture and tradition. In fact, the real beauty and meaning of these idols are only apparent when they are seen in this context.

It is not enough to end the plunder of our antiquities. We need to let our gods return home. The only sensible way to prevent future theft is to document them carefully in a publicly accessible National Antiquities Register. A properly documented artefact is worth little in the international black market and consequently much less likely to be stolen.

(This piece was originally published in *Hindustan Times*, November 2016)

# WHY WE MUST WRITE OUR OWN STORY

One is often told that Indians do not care for their history. This is an odd accusation to hurl at a people who have a fair claim to being the world's oldest civilisation. Millions of Indians start their day with Bronze Age chants and everyday conversations are peppered with allusions to Iron Age epics. Even our politics is impacted by who did or did not pull down a temple in the sixteenth century. If anything, we Indians are obsessed with history. Perhaps what we do not really care about is the stuff in textbooks.

The problem is that the official history contained in our textbooks simply does not ring true for most Indians. First of all, it is quite amazing the extent to which colonial-era prejudices have been perpetuated to this day. More overt biases such as the blatantly racist Aryan Invasion Theory has been challenged, but many others remain embedded. For instance, we routinely term Chanakya as 'Machiavellian' and Samudra Gupta as the 'Napoleon of India'.

It may appear that calling someone 'Napoleon' is a

compliment, but even a casual deconstruction of these epithets shows that colonial historians meant something totally different. Remember that the British were proud that they had defeated Napoleon repeatedly—so the real message to an Indian audience was that Samudra Gupta may have been a great general, but the British would still have defeated him. As the African saying goes, 'Until the lions have their own story-teller, history will always glorify the hunter.'

Rather than systematically remove colonial prejudices, post-Independence historians added an additional layer. Quite apart from the political preferences of the Nehruvians and Marxists, the narrative came to be dominated by Delhi as if the rest of the country must exist as mere provinces. Thus, we are told of obscure Delhi-based dynasties like the Lodhis, but virtually nothing about the Vijayanagar empire, the Deccan sultans or the Ahoms of Assam.

Delhi's monopoly has introduced a peculiar inland bias that ignores the country's extraordinary maritime past. Thus, it is possible to grow up in India without hearing anything about the exploits of ancient Odiya mariners, the links of the Cholas and Pallavas to South-East Asia or Indo-Roman trade. This is rather like retelling European history without mentioning Athens, Venice, Portugal, Spain and England.

The landlocked mindset has a real impact on how we engage with the world. Coastal history is about exploration, risk-taking and external orientation, whereas Delhi views the outside world as the perpetual source of invaders. In turn, this has influenced our economic and foreign policy. For example, India's geopolitical approach is entirely dominated by China and Pakistan. From a maritime perspective, however, Oman and Indonesia are our close neighbours. A more balanced historical narrative would tell us of our close ties to these countries over thousands of years. Indeed, the Indonesians take so much pride in our civilisational links that they named their country and their currency after ours! Even their national airline is named Garuda after Vishnu's *vahana* or vehicle, the eagle. Contrast this with Pakistan's official policy of erasing its links to the Indic civilisation. On whom should we spend our diplomatic energy?

Another major problem with Indian history writing is the disdain for evidence. Historical facts are not static since new discoveries are constantly thrown up by archaeology, genetics, climate sciences, and so on. As with all fields of knowledge, existing hypotheses need to be tested against new evidence.

Note that I am not complaining here about differences in interpretation. When people can argue so vociferously about current events, it is not surprising that historians disagree on thousand-year-old events. The real problem is that so much personal and sometimes political capital gets invested in certain narratives, that evidence is seldom updated. Quoting authority is seen as more important than primary material.

This problem is not unique to either India or history writing. As the physicist Max Plank famously said, 'Science progresses one funeral at a time.' The problem is that it takes more than one funeral in a country with a strong tradition of perpetuating dynasty and 'guru-shishya parampara'. The disdain for facts, in turn, has discouraged the systematic collation of primary evidence. Reports of major archaeological digs are left incomplete and key artefacts are often untraceable, perhaps stolen.

These are a few of the problems facing Indian history writing. Note that I have deliberately avoided getting into ideological and political debates. I think correcting the above three distortions should be acceptable to serious scholars from across the ideological spectrum. Quite apart from removing major distortions, it will have two important benefits. First, it will make history more about exploration and discovery than about memorising a static narrative. Second, it will give Indians a feeling of ownership over their own story and a broader worldview.

(This piece was originally published in *Hindustan Times*, August 2016)

# WHY PM'S INDEPENDENCE DAY SPEECH SHOULD MOVE OUT OF DELHI

There is a big difference in the way 15 August and 26 January are celebrated. The former is led by the Prime Minister's speech from the ramparts of Delhi's Red Fort, while the latter by a grand military parade on Rajpath overseen by the President. Most people accept this difference as merely the artifact of tradition, but the ceremonies carry important symbolism. In this column I suggest an innovation that would make the symbolism more appropriate and meaningful.

As all Indians are aware, Republic Day commemorates the date on which the Indian Constitution came into effect. In other words, it is a celebration of the Indian State and the power that resides in it by virtue of the Constitution. The Mauryan lions, our State emblem, reflect this power. It is appropriate, therefore, that Republic Day celebrations are led by military parades on Rajpath and that the President, as head of the Republic, presides over the event. It is a top-down show of strength and the national capital is the obvious place from which the celebrations are led.

Independence Day, in contrast, is a commemoration of the day we became free of British rule. By its very nature, it is a bottom-up celebration of freedom and belongs to the people rather than the Indian State. Therefore, the Prime Minister, as representative of the people, leads the celebrations with a speech. However, note that neither the national capital nor Red Fort have any special place in it beyond tradition. Freedom belongs equally to residents of the smallest village in Meghalaya or Kerala. This is why the symbolic importance of Independence Day would be greatly enhanced if the Prime Minister would deliver his annual speech from a different location every year.

There are many locations across India that have strong historical associations with the idea of freedom. Here are a few suggestions that could be considered:

## CHITTAURGARH, RAJASTHAN

Few places on earth have a history of such heroic resistance against external aggression. The fort was ransacked three times (in 1303 by Alauddin Khilji; by Bahadur Shah in1535; by Akbar in 1567) and on each occasion it was defended to the last man. Each time, the women chose to commit mass-suicides than live in slavery and dishonour. Even after the fall of the fort, the people of Mewar kept up the resistance in the surrounding Aravalli hills.

## JHANSI, UP

This town and its fort will forever be linked to the brave resistance of Rani Lakshmibai to British domination. Given how the events of 1857–58 are immortalised in poetry and song, would it not be appropriate if Prime Minister Modi delivered this year's speech from the same spot where the young queen is said to have leapt off the fort's ramparts in order to escape the siege?

## COLACHEL, TAMIL NADU

This is the coastal town where Martanda Varma, ruler of the tiny kingdom of Venad (later Travancore) decisively defeated the Dutch East India Company in 1741. This was a major feat as the Dutch were then the world's leading maritime power and controlled what is now South Africa, Indonesia and Sri Lanka. The Dutch never recovered and went into decline. No Asian would again defeat a European power decisively till the Japanese navy defeated the Russians at the Battle of Tsushima in 1905. A commemorative column still stands at the spot where Martanda Varma accepted Dutch surrender.

## SARAIGHAT, ASSAM

Indian history is full of invasions from the north-west but almost none from the north-east. For this we should thank the Assamese and the Manipuris who put up extraordinary resistance to foreign marauders such as the Burmese. Even when foreign invaders from the north-west managed to reach

Assam, they were defeated. Bakhtiyar Khilji, who ransacked Nalanda and conquered Bengal, was soundly defeated by the Assamese. Similarly, when Aurangzeb sent a large army to subdue the Assamese in 1671, the Ahom general Lachit Borphukan enticed the Mughals into a naval battle on the Brahmaputra and sank their fleet. This battle took place at Saraighat, not far from modern Guwahati.

## THE CELLULAR JAIL, ANDAMAN & NICOBAR ISLANDS (KALA PANI)

In the late nineteenth and early twentieth centuries, the British used the Cellular Jail in Port Blair to imprison those whom it considered the greatest threats to the continuation of colonial rule. Its inmates included, Maulvi Liaquat Ali, the Savarkar brothers, Sachindra Nath Sanyal, Barindra Ghosh and many others.

The above list contains mere suggestions and readers are free to add others. Of course, the Prime Minister may return to the Red Fort from time to time. The main point is that Independence Day does not belong exclusively to Delhi and should be shared across India. This would fit the spirit of freedom much better than the current ritual.

(This piece was originally published in *Hindustan Times*, January 2017)

# I AM ANCHORED BY IDEAS

**Q: Childhood's best moment?**

A: After I finished my class 10 board exams, I went trekking in Sikkim with two of my closest friends. We were sixteen and we travelled on local buses, trudged up steep mountain paths and stayed in remote villages. It was the first taste of being completely free. That taste for adventure has never quite left me. I still go walking in the mountains, sometimes alone.

**Q: Education trajectory?**

A: The very first school I attended was kindergarten in a small Bahai school in Gangtok; I believe it is still there. I later attended St. Xavier's and St. James' schools in Kolkata before heading to Shri Ram College of Commerce in Delhi. I then got the Rhodes Scholarship which allowed me to attend Oxford University.

**Q: Favourite dessert?**

A: *Nalen gurer rasogolla.* These are not the chewy, white

ones you get commonly (which I dislike), but the brown ones you get in Kolkata only in winter. And then there are hot jalebis in the lanes of Varanasi.

## Q: What were your childhood dreams?

A: I did not have any specific childhood dreams, certainly never thought that I would be a bestselling writer or become the Principal Economic Adviser to the Indian Government. I am anchored by ideas, values and relationships, not by personal life goals. So, I have lived life as an adventure and let it take me wherever it does. I have no idea where I will be at fifty.

## Q: Favourite movie?

A: Like many of my generation, *Sholay* is a childhood favourite. More recent favourites would include *Three Idiots* and *Bhaag Milkha Bhaag*. A Hollywood favourite is *Master and Commander*, a film that fed into my interest in maritime history. Let's say, slow-moving art films, shot in shades of grey, are not my thing.

## Q: First job?

A: My scholarship money at Oxford came to an end in mid-1995 and I was wondering what to do next. This was when I got an interview call from Crosby Securities in Singapore. I had never heard of the company, never been to Singapore and had no idea about the job of a financial sector economist, but they sent me a first-class ticket! Since I had never been to Singapore, I decided to take the chance and, as it happened, got the job. That is how I became a financial markets' economist.

**Q: Have you found yourself in a difficult situation?**

A:I have often found myself in difficult situations: being sucked into quicksand, being robbed while backpacking in Guatemala, being stuck in a savanna wildfire in Africa and so on. I am quite good at getting myself into trouble.

**Q: What terrifies you?**

A: I do fear the prospect of spending an evening watching a slow-moving art film, or attending a book-reading of some pretentious literary novel. For some odd reason, I keep getting invited to such events—perhaps people assume that a Bengali writer must like these things.

**Q: What are your hobbies?**

A: I have many hobbies and interests. I play several sports, including being a Taekwondo black belt. I also love to read, travel, climb over old ruins, follow old maps and investigate the underbellies of cities. Those who read my books and columns will already have a taste this.

**Q: One piece of advice for youngsters...**

A: There are many ways to live life. One can live life by single-mindedly following dreams and goals, or by following a process, or by letting life flow by itself. Each path has its pros and cons. One must decide what works for you and take the plunge. What matters is being able to live with the consequences of one's decisions. Resilience counts more than meticulous planning.

**Q: How to handle work-life balance?**

A: I have always done multiple things simultaneously. As you can tell, I mix all kinds of interests, hobbies, demanding careers and family obligations. Nonetheless, I ensure that I only have one thing with hard deadlines at any time. In other words, one activity clearly takes priority—at present it's my role as Principal Economic Adviser to the Indian government. Everything else adjusts around it.

**Q: Favourite author?**

A: I have very eclectic reading habits. My favourite non-fiction writers include, Ryszard Kapuscinski, a Polish journalist who wrote wonderful first-hand accounts of several important events of the late twentieth century. Then there is Peter Hopkirk who has written excellent histories of European explorers and their exploits in Central Asia. My favourite fiction writers range from Hemingway to Amish Tripathi. One thing common to all these writers is that they use direct language and keep the narrative flowing, something I try to achieve in my own writing style. I strongly dislike flowery language, vague plots and excessive use of stylistic devices.

**Q: What is the best food you have ever tasted?**

A: This is really difficult since I love variety and have many favourites. Internationally, Singapore is perhaps the world's best place to eat out—the pepper crab is my all-time favourite. Much is made of the food scene in London, Paris and New York, but Asian cities like Tokyo and Shanghai are now far ahead. Kolkata may have lost its crown in other fields, but it is still India's culinary capital—it has some great restaurants, street vendors and home-cooked food. However, every Indian state has great culinary traditions. I am pleased to see that we are moving away from generic 'Indian' restaurants to more specialised regional food.

**Q: What's life after retirement?**

A: Retirement? I have no intention of ever retiring—there are so many things to do, so many books to write....

(This interview was originally published in *The Economic Times*, July 2017)

# ONCE UPON A RIVER

In the year 1671, the Ahom kingdom (roughly, modern Assam, now) faced a crisis. A huge Mughal army was making its way from Bengal and threatening to completely overwhelm it. For the previous two generations, the Assamese had been under continuous pressure from the Mughals, but had used diplomacy and guerrilla tactics to hold off the invaders—but it looked like their time was up.

A decade earlier, in 1661, Emperor Aurganzeb had sent a large force under Mir Jumla to attack the Ahom kingdom. The Assamese had been defeated repeatedly in open battles and had to surrender their capital, but had kept up the guerrilla resistance. Mir Jumla had eventually been forced to withdraw, but not before having imposed humiliating conditions on the tiny kingdom. The Assamese did not forget this, and they gradually began clawing back territory. Eventually in December 1667, Aurangzeb decided to teach them a lesson and sent a huge army complete with

Turkic and Rajput cavalry and, most importantly, heavy cannons.

The Ahom army was led by a dynamic general, Lachit Borphukan, but his army was a fraction of the Mughal forces. He knew that he would be decimated on an open terrain. So he built defences in the hills near Guwahati and using deception, kept buying time. Although he was losing men in skirmishes and knew that his soldiers were demoralised, he kept up the effort. Legend has it that Borphukan even publicly decapitated his maternal uncle for being negligent.

Eventually, in March 1671, the Ahom general managed to entice the Mughals into a naval battle on the Brahmaputra river, where the latter couldn't have used their cavalry. The overconfident Mughals had heavy boats arrayed with artillery, but they proved no match for the small, manoeuvrable Assamese boats. Although severely ill, Borphukan personally led the attack and won a great naval battle, not unlike that won by the Greeks against the Persians at Salamis. Thus, it was the Assamese—and not the Marathas or Bundelas as is often assumed—who inflicted the first major defeat on the Mughal empire.

This major turning point in Indian history took place at Saraighat, not far from Guwahati. There is a big modern bridge spanning the Brahmaputra there, with a small memorial across the river commemorating the battle.

The Brahmaputra is one of the great rivers of Asia. It originates from a glacier 100 kilometres south-east of Manasarovar and initially flows east across the Tibetan plateau. At this stage, the river is known as Tsangpo. It then turns south, cutting through the Himalayas in a series of spectacular and raging gorges, to enter Arunachal Pradesh, where it is known as Dihang or Siang.

The river then enters the plains near the picturesque town of Pasighat. As it enters the plains of Assam, the river takes on the name Brahmaputra (Brahma's son), which is most familiar to Indians. At this stage, the river slows down and spreads out. Indeed, there are stretches where it is more than eight kilometres wide. In the seventeenth century, floods and tectonic movements created the island of Majuli in the middle of the river, which was till recently the largest river island in the world. Majuli would acquire great cultural significance for the Assamese, but unfortunately the river is now steadily eroding the island away.

After Majuli, the river flows past Kaziranga National Park, famous for its rhinos, and the city of Guwahati, before flowing into Bangladesh. Here, it is called Jamuna before it merges with the Padma distributary of the Ganga to form the world's largest delta. From its point of origin till it combines with the Ganga, the Brahmaputra is about 2,900 kilometres long. Nonetheless, it is interesting to note that despite its size and cultural and economic importance, it was not known till the late nineteenth century that the Tsangpo and the Brahmaputra were the same river.

In the late nineteenth century, the British were secretly mapping out Tibet using surveyor-spies like the legendary Nain Singh. The Tibetan authorities were suspicious of British intentions, so the surveys had to be done in utmost secrecy. Singh's surveys had raised an important geographical question—where did the Tsangpo flow? Was it, as he suggested, linked to the Brahmaputra?

In 1880, the Survey of India decided to send out a team comprising a Chinese lama and a Sikkimese surveyor called Kinthup. Unfortunately, the lama was more interested in having a good time and the team was stuck for four months in a village, where the lama decided to spend his time drinking and seducing the headman's daughter. They finally fled after the affair became known. Things did not improve even when they finally entered Tibet. The lama sold Kinthup as a slave and disappeared. Kinthup had to spend nearly a year (May 1881–March 1882) working as a slave before escaping to a monastery to become a novice monk.

Then, after several months, he asked for permission to go on a pilgrimage and instead, went up to the banks of the Tsangpo where he cut 500 logs of regular length and hid them in a cave before returning. Several months later, he again asked for permission to make a pilgrimage to Lhasa. Meanwhile, he sent a message back to the Survey that he would throw fifty logs a day into the Tsangpo, as had been agreed.

Kinthup did as he had promised but the message did not reach the Survey in time. He had been presumed lost or dead and the watch on the Brahmaputra had been abandoned. Thus, no one saw the logs floating down the river and poor Kinthup never got the recognition he deserved for his extraordinary efforts. He would live out his last days as a tailor in Darjeeling. Later, surveys would confirm that the Tsangpo and the Brahmaputra were the same.

(This piece was originally published in *The Indian Express*, April 2014)

# THE LAST PAGANS OF IRAQ

With US President Barack Obama belatedly ordering air strikes and humanitarian airdrops of food and relief supplies to refugees in northern Iraq, the world is finally taking action against the Islamic State. Within a few months, the jihadist group, which until recently called itself the Islamic State in Iraq and Syria, has taken control of large parts of both countries, where it has proclaimed a new Caliphate. But the real reason to fear the Islamic State is not its lust for power; it is the systematic, cold-blooded way in which its members are erasing the region's social, cultural, and demographic past.

Within a few weeks, the Islamic State has virtually eliminated the entire Shia Muslim, and Christian populations from the lands that it controls. The city of Mosul, home to one of the world's oldest Christian communities, no longer has any Christians left. Priceless Assyrian artifacts have been publicly destroyed in a campaign against idolatry.

Indeed, the Islamic State has not even spared Sunni

co-religionists who do not adhere to their extreme interpretation of Islam. A number of revered shrines have been demolished, including one said to be the Tomb of Jonah. As terrible as all of this is, the worst of the persecution has been aimed at the Yezidi, an ancient religious group that lives among the Kurds. They number less than half a million, and two-thirds of them live around Mosul in northern Iraq. The rest are scattered across neighbouring countries like Syria, Armenia, and Turkey. The more recent immigrant communities are to be found in Germany and the United States.

Although influenced over the centuries by Christianity and Islam, the Yezidi religion has ancient pagan roots that go back at least to the late Bronze Age. Interestingly, their beliefs have many similarities with Hinduism—for example, they believe in reincarnation, say their prayers facing the sun at sunrise and sunset, and even have a caste system. They also worship Tawûsê-Melek, the peacock angel—a bird that is found in the Indian subcontinent but not in Yezidi lands.

While the origins of the Yezidi are uncertain, cultural and genetic evidence suggests that they may be the distant remnants of Indian tribes that migrated west in the second millennium BC. There is considerable evidence of Indian links with the Middle East during the Bronze Age. For example, Zoroastrianism, the religion of ancient Iran—to which Yezidi religious beliefs have been linked—is closely related to early Hinduism.

Over the centuries, both Christians and Muslims dubbed

the Yezidi 'devil worshippers', and subjected them to relentless persecution, which was especially extreme under the Ottoman Turks in the eighteenth and nineteenth centuries. A series of massacres killed hundreds of thousands and almost led to their extinction.

Under Saddam Hussein, the Yezidi were not subjected to overt religious persecution, though they remained under pressure to Arabise their culture. Matters have since taken a turn for the worse. In April 2007, gunmen dragged twenty-three Yezidi men from a bus and shot them dead. Four months later, a series of coordinated car-bomb attacks killed at least 300 more, including women and children.

The Yezidis now face their greatest crisis ever. The Islamic State gave the Christians of Mosul the choice to convert, pay the *jizya* (a special tax levied on non-Muslims under Sharia law), or leave. The Yezidi have been given no such choice and are killed on sight as devil worshippers.

The Yezidi heartland around Mosul is now largely under the Islamic State's control. The small town of Sinjar, the only place in the world with a Yezidi majority, fell in the first few days of August as Kurdish fighters were forced to withdraw. Reports of large-scale massacres are trickling in. Many refugees escaped into the mountains, where they are trapped in shrinking enclaves. Hundreds are said to have died already of thirst and starvation. The most sacred Yezidi pilgrimage site at Lalish runs the risk of being demolished.

Sadly, there has been little media outrage at the predicament faced by the Yezidis. Perhaps the US airdrops and promised strategic interventions, together with a possible coordinated operation by Kurdish forces (rearmed by the US), may rescue the survivors, but it appears unlikely that they will be able to return to their homes soon.

Centuries ago, the last Zoroastrians fled persecution in Iran for India. Their descendants, the tiny Parsi community, still live there. Today, who will give refuge to the last pagans of Iraq?

(This piece was originally published in *Project Syndicate*, August 2014)

# THE FORGOTTEN GENOCIDE

It is exactly forty years since the Pakistani military regime of Yahya Khan initiated 'Operation Searchlight' in March 1971. That military expedition was but the latest in a series of pogroms carried out to intimidate the restive population of what was then called East Pakistan—today's independent Bangladesh. What followed was one of the worst massacres in human history, now all but forgotten by the international community.

Pakistan was created after the partition of British India in 1947, but its territory was divided into two enclaves separated by hundreds of miles. While they shared a religion, Islam, there were major cultural and linguistic differences between East and West Pakistan.

In the east, there was a strong sense of being Bengali, and a sizeable Hindu minority continued to live in the province. There was, moreover, strong resentment that political power lay in the hands of politicians and generals of West Pakistan who were blatantly insensitive towards the

Bengalis. It appeared as if with the creation of Pakistan, East Pakistan had merely exchanged one form of colonialism for another. And, as the Bengali demand for autonomy gained momentum, the response became more repressive.

In November 1970, a tropical cyclone named 'Bhola' struck East Pakistan, killing between 300,000–500,000 people. Bhola is still considered one of the worst natural disasters on record, and the military dictatorship's lukewarm relief efforts incensed the Bengali population even more.

So, when Pakistan's military leaders finally allowed elections in late December 1970, East Pakistan voted overwhelmingly for the Bengali-nationalist Awami League party, which won 167 out of 169 seats in the province. Since East Pakistan was more populous than West Pakistan, the election's outcome raised the prospect of Bengalis ruling the country as a whole. This was not palatable to the Punjabi-dominated military brass or to Zulfikar Ali Bhutto, the leader of West Pakistan's largest political party. The elections were cancelled, and East Pakistan erupted in an open revolt.

Yahya Khan responded by sending in troops. The result was a genocide in which as many as three million people, particularly minorities and intellectuals, were killed. Dhaka University's residential halls were particularly targeted—up to 700 students were killed in a single attack on Jagannath Hall. Several well-known professors, both Hindu and Muslim, were murdered. Hundreds of thousands of women were systematically raped in the countryside. By September 1971, ten million refugees had poured into eastern India.

The world knew what was happening. *Time* magazine's

2 August 1971 issue quoted a United States official saying, 'This is the most incredible, calculated thing since the days of the Nazis in Poland.' The article went on to describe the stream of refugees:

> Over the rivers and down the highways and along countless jungle paths, the population of East Pakistan continues to hemorrhage into India: an endless unorganized flow of refugees with a few tin kettles, cardboard boxes, and ragged clothes piled on their heads, carrying their sick children and their old. They pad along barefooted, with the mud sucking at their heels in the wet parts. They are silent, except for a child whimpering now and then, but their faces tell the story. Many are sick and covered with sores. Others have cholera, and when they die by the roadside there is no one to bury them.

The international community's response to the massacres was shameful. We now have copies of desperate cables sent by diplomat Archer Blood and his colleagues at the US consulate in Dacca (now Dhaka) pleading with the US government to stop supporting a military regime that was carrying out genocide. Instead, President Richard Nixon concentrated on intimidating Indian Prime Minister Indira Gandhi into staying out. He would even send the US Seventh Fleet to cow her down. Fortunately, Gandhi held her nerve and began to prepare for war.

Strengthened by promises of support from the US and China, Pakistan's military commanders ordered pre-emptive air strikes against India on 3 December 1971. The Indian response was swift and sharp. With support from the civilian population, as well as from the Mukti Bahini, an irregular army of Bengali rebels, the Indian army swept into East Pakistan. Nixon was too bogged down in Vietnam to do more than issue threats. On 16 December, the Pakistanis signed the instrument of surrender in Dacca. Bangladesh was born.

Having acquiesced in the genocide, the international community has conveniently forgotten it, and no Pakistani official has ever been brought to justice. On the contrary, many of the perpetrators later held senior government positions. It is as if the Nuremberg trials never happened after the Second World War.

As the world watches Libya's Muammar el-Qaddafi slaughter his own people, we should remember the human cost of international indifference.

(This piece was originally published in *Project Syndicate*, March 2011)

# INDIA'S ELITES IN CRISIS

For a country with 1.2 billion people, India is ruled by a surprisingly small elite, which runs everything from the government to large companies and even sports bodies. But a series of scandals, some involving billions of dollars, has now seriously undermined that elite's standing in the eyes of the Indian public.

Almost anyone in a position of power in India, including well-known print and television journalists, is now viewed with suspicion. This is occurring at a time when economic growth is pulling a young and upwardly mobile population into the urban middle class. This new middle class is no longer constrained by the patronage systems of the village, but it also does not enjoy the cosy relationship that links the old middle class with the elite. Could this crisis of the elite trigger India's own Tiananmen Square moment?

Except in totalitarian regimes, a country's elite depends on a degree of popular acceptance, which is mostly derived from the belief that the elite is broadly 'fair' in its dealings.

Following the recent series of scandals, the average Indian does not believe this anymore.

Of course, doubts about the ruling elite are not unique to India. Almost all countries undergoing a shift from a pre-industrial equilibrium based on patronage to one based on modern institutions and the rule of law have faced such crises of legitimacy.

Until the early nineteenth century, for example, British politics was extraordinarily corrupt. The old aristocracy not only dominated the House of Lords, but also used its influence to get relatives, friends and family retainers elected to the House of Commons by exploiting a key institutional weakness—the existence of 'rotten boroughs' that could be bought and sold.

The Duke of Newcastle alone is said to have controlled seven such boroughs, each with two representatives. Meanwhile, large and populous industrial cities such as Birmingham and Manchester were barely represented. In 1819, a crowd of 60,000 gathered in Manchester to demand reform, but were charged by the cavalry. Fifteen people were killed and many more injured in what is remembered as the Peterloo Massacre.

Given the recent memory of the violent French Revolution, the British elite reluctantly agreed to democratising reforms. Ultimately, the Reform Act of 1832 abolished the rotten boroughs and extended the franchise to the new middle class (the working class and women would have to wait).

The United States, too, went through a period of robber

baron industrialisation in the 1870s and 1880s. The greed and corruption of that era were satirised in 1873 by Mark Twain and Charles Dudley Warner in their book, *The Gilded Age: A Tale of Today*. The period ended with the depression of 1893-96, and was followed by the major political reforms of the Progressive Era.

For Britain and the US, the transition in the nature of the governing elite was relatively smooth. But there are many examples where such change was sudden and violent—the French and Russian revolutions, for example. In Germany, the Prussian elite successfully managed the country's industrialisation in the late nineteenth century, but was discredited by defeat in the First World War. Nazism filled the ensuing vacuum, and a new order would be established only after the Second World War.

Similar shifts have been witnessed in Asia. Japan saw two shifts—the Meiji Restoration of 1868 and the period after the Second World War. South Korea was ruled by generals until widespread student protests led to a democratic transition in 1987. (Many of the country's top businessmen faced prosecution in subsequent years.) Indonesia experienced its shift more recently, in 1998.

When China confronted this moment during the Tiananmen Square protests of 1989, the communist state repressed the students with an iron fist, but has since maintained a single-minded focus on economic growth. Corruption remains a major problem, but the authorities take care to punish the worst excesses in a highly visible way. Still, as the recent controversy over the Nobel Peace Prize demonstrated, the government remains nervous about any dissent that challenges the legitimacy of the ruling elite.

Even adjusted for purchasing power, India's middle class today probably totals no more than seventy million (far smaller than is generally assumed). But, in the coming decade, today's established middle class will be swamped by newcomers working their way up from the country's slums, small towns and villages.

One can see them everywhere—learning English in coaching centres, working anonymously in the new malls and call centres, or suddenly famous as sports stars. Never before has India experienced such social mobility. So far, this new group has been too busy climbing the income ladder to express their resentment at the excesses of the elite, but one can feel a growing sense of anger among its members.

It is impossible to predict when the shift will happen or what form it will take. Given India's democratic traditions, it is likely that the change will be peaceful. One possibility is that it will take place province by province—the previously ungovernable state of Bihar being a prime example.

But we may also see an unpredictable turn, with a new political leader or movement suddenly capturing the popular imagination and sweeping aside the old arrangements. As we know from Nazi Germany, Soviet Russia and other cases, such movements do not always lead to a happy outcome.

Perhaps India's existing elite will learn from history, purge itself, and then open itself up to new talent. Many investigations have been ordered into the current corruption scandals. Over the course of this year, Indians will find out if such efforts are serious and whether they will lead to reform—or merely to deeper crisis.

(This piece was originally published in *Project Syndicate*, January 2011)

# TAMING INDIA'S ELITE

It has been more than a year and a half since Prime Minister Narendra Modi came to power on a promise to build a new India, one founded on a radical break with the past.

It is still too early to gauge the impact of his economic and foreign policies, but there is one area where his government is making palpable progress: taming India's entrenched elite.

India has a population of 1.2 billion people, but it has long been dominated by a tiny elite: a couple of hundred extended families, totalling perhaps 4,000 to 5,000 people. Many countries have powerful elites with outsize influence but, in India, dynastic elites control the top echelons in every sphere of public life: politics, business, the media, and even Bollywood.

Many of these dynasties have roots that stretch back to the colonial era, implying at least seven decades of dominance. Every point of leverage—from government contracts and industrial licences to national awards—is used to maintain this ecosystem of power.

Over time, ties of patronage and marriage have fused these dynasties into a discernible class, concentrated in central New Delhi, with a few pockets in Mumbai and a small presence in other parts of the country. Exclusive English-language schools, holiday homes in Goa, and summers in London or Switzerland have given them a shared worldview.

Occasionally, new faces are admitted, but only if they do not interfere with the system's perpetuation.

Unsurprisingly, the result has been the creation of a class of people with a strong sense of entitlement, who react to even minor challenges by closing ranks. They flaunt their power so often (usually with some variant of the phrase, 'Do you not know who I am?') that even those who do not 'belong' sometimes use similar lines to try to bluff their way out of trouble.

One of Mr Modi's more symbolic blows to the old establishment has been his government's success in evicting high-status squatters from hundreds of government bungalows in central Delhi.

Few of the occupants of these sprawling official residences had the right to live in them. In some cases, they had been there for generations; when faced with eviction notices, some families argued that the bungalows had effectively become memorials to their famous ancestors and that they should thus be allowed to remain.

An even more visible change is the sudden increase in criminal charges—ranging from corruption to sexual offences—being filed against members of the old elite. The homes of several senior civil servants have been raided recently as part of corruption investigations, and serious accusations of sexual harassment have been levelled against India's top environmentalist, Dr Rajendra Pachauri, who headed the United Nations Intergovernmental Panel on Climate Change when it received the Nobel Peace Prize.

Meanwhile, banks have begun to demand repayment from large borrowers accustomed to having their loans rolled over. Vijay Mallya, a businessman famous for his colourful lifestyle and string of failed ventures, is being investigated as a willful defaulter.

Much of this would have been unthinkable until a few months ago. And, inevitably, many accuse the government of carrying out political vendettas. On 19 December, Sonia Gandhi, the then president of the Congress party, and her son Rahul Gandhi (now, president of the party), were forced to appear in court on corruption charges. In response, their party's MPs brought legislative activity to a halt for days. The two were quickly released on bail.

The case against the Gandhis—as well as many other high-profile investigations—is likely to drag on for years. And, of course, in some cases the accused will be exonerated. But the very fact that members of the old elite can be investigated and questioned is undeniable progress in a country where they have long enjoyed impunity.

What remains to be seen is whether Mr Modi is able to cement these gains. The elite can be remarkably resilient, retaining the power to strike back at the first sign of weakness. History—from post-revolutionary France to modern Thailand—has repeatedly shown that it is a mistake to write off the old establishment.

(This piece was originally published in *Project Syndicate*, January 2016)

# WHY MUNNI IS INFAMOUS IN INDIA

Three weeks ago, a khap panchayat (caste council) in Bhenswal village, Uttar Pradesh, issued a diktat banning girls from wearing jeans. They argued that jeans 'encouraged' couples to elope! This is no isolated incident. In the last couple of years, a number of colleges have attempted to ban their female students from wearing jeans. However, this ire against jeans is not about a piece of apparel, but about rapidly changing socio-cultural attitudes. The combination of urbanisation, rising incomes, cable television and mobile telephony is liquefying Indian society at an unprecedented rate. The ban in Bhenswal village, therefore, does not reflect the growing power of caste councils, but a losing rear-guard action by an older generation unable to deal with such rapid change.

The clothes worn by the Indian male have been shifting to trousers and shirts since the late nineteenth century. It has been a slow, but steady transformation and is far from complete. For reasons of convenience or style, many Indian men still wear traditional clothes in daily life. Still, it is fair to say that Western attire is common enough even in the remotest villages to be now considered unremarkable. The story for women is different.

Till recently, Indian women largely continued to wear traditional clothes. Usually this implied the sari, although some states had other local attires (for instance, the *mekhla-sador* in Assam). The wearing of western outfits was rare except for the upper and upper-middle classes in large cities. The first sign of change was the gradual shift from the late 1970s to the salwar-kameez, a dress that was originally from the north-west of the country. By the 1990s, its different variants became the dress of choice for young urban women across the country. Now, we are witnessing a second and much faster change. In the last two years, I have travelled from Ladakh to Tamil Nadu, and from Gujarat to the North-East. The trends are clear. In small mofussil towns and even in villages, unmarried teenage girls increasingly wear jeans. Most will still shift to traditional clothes after marriage, but it is only a matter of time before that too will not be a barrier.

One could lament the homogenising effects of globalisation on local culture. It is not for me to pass judgement. However, jeans are a reflection of a deeper transformation in social attitudes, aspirations and even gender equations. Perhaps it is inevitable with literacy, rising incomes, urbanisation, access to mobile telephony, trends in Bollywood and exposure to cable television. Moreover, it shows through in many other facets of life. The thirst to learn the English language is yet another manifestation of the phenomenon. We can see it everywhere—in English-medium schools in the slums and villages, language-learning channels on cable TV, and 'guide books' sold at street-corners. Politicians may cry foul, but India's poor are voting with their feet.

There may be temptation to interpret the above trends as westernisation. However, there are many ways in which the trends point the other way. Take popular music for example. Till the mid-Nineties, the urban middle class listened to a fair amount of American and British music in addition to local popular music. The older readers will recall Cliff Richards, the Beatles, Michael Jackson and Madonna. Today, one hardly hears a Western tune. Instead, rural migrants are bringing their own tastes from the hinterland that find expression in superhits like *Munni badnaam hui* (literally, Munni became infamous) and *Beedi jalai le* (literally, come on, light a beedi). An earlier generation of Bollywood songwriters would have blushed at the lusty lyrics. But it's now considered cool.

Similarly, the new middle-class that is emerging from the urbanisation process has a very different relationship with the English language than the pre-existing middle-class. To the new group, English is just a skill necessary to climb the job market. In contrast, the language was about a whole culture for the old middle-class. Great pride was once taken in speaking 'propah' English and quoting Shakespeare. Hardly anyone cares now. The point is that the new India has the confidence to absorb outside influences on its own terms.

The change in attitude is feeding through even to Indians who live abroad. The lonely and alienated immigrant described by American-Indian writers like Jhumpa Lahiri no longer rings true for most expatriate Indians of today. Indeed, the fate of the US green card is a good illustration of how things have changed. Less than a decade ago, the acquisition of a US green card would be a matter of great celebration for a Non-Resident Indian (NRI). Parents back home would proudly announce to their friends and relatives if their child obtained one. The trend has completely reversed at least for the upper and upper-middle class. Successful global Indians now go out of their way to give up their green cards in order to avoid paying US taxes. This would have been unthinkable ten years ago.

Such rapid changes in our social and cultural attitudes will inevitably have repercussions. The diktats of khap panchayats and clerics are only an extreme illustration of this. There are grumblings about the 'Bollywoodisation' of our culture. Language purists lament the mish-mash vocabulary of the youth. There is a genuine danger that many local dialects and customs will disappear. However, the process can no longer be reversed. Love it or hate it, the new India is here to stay.

(This piece was originally published in *Business Standard*, February 2011)

# URBAN DYNAMICS

The CAS framework is a particularly useful way to think about cities. Its many variants are widely used consciously or unconsciously for managing cities around the world. Sadly, this is still new in India where architecture and urban-related thinking continues to be dominated by the mid-twentieth century ideas of Le Corbusier and socialist brutalism. A Cartesian ideal imposed by a rigid master plan is seen as the best way to manage cities despite the fact that this approach has been a total failure for half a century. This point is brought out in the first couple of essays in this section.

So what does the CAS advocate? The reader who has read the previous section titled, *History & Culture* will by now be familiar with the advocacy of a flexible, organic approach. However, let me take the opportunity to introduce a new concept—'strange attractors'. I have not used this term in any of the pieces due to concerns that it would have put off the average reader, but it is key to policy interventions using the CAS approach. At the risk of oversimplification, think of the strange attractor as a node in a complex system that manages to drive the dynamics of a 'basin' around itself. Thus, urban authorities do not try to prescriptively plan the whole system, but use strategic interventions to introduce/ enhance such attractors that lead to a certain outcome (while constantly monitoring whether or not it is spiraling off in an unintended direction).

The essays in this section include several examples of strange attractors that can be used by city managers to create positive dynamics. One example that I have quoted is that of a world class maritime museum in Mumbai as an anchor institution. The same idea is presented more generally in terms of using universities and intellectual clusters to drive human capital agglomeration in cities.

One of the innovative ways in which we can use this approach is to rethink slums as strange attractors that act as 'routers' in the migration process. In other words, Indian slums are not static places of despair as popularly believed, but a first rung in the socio-economic ladder. Indeed, the idea of a social ladder has important implications for how we set up public housing, and property rights. This is also a useful framework for understanding the way urban villages within the city evolve over time. Of course, these are merely illustrative and there are many other ways in which the CAS approach can be applied.

# THE IDEOLOGY OF CITIES

It is often not recognised that all cities are ultimately a reflection of some underlying ideology that not only is a theoretical influence but, as we shall see, has a very real impact on the way a city functions and evolves. A dysfunctional or outdated urban philosophy will lead to a dysfunctional or stagnant city. Successful cities around the world consciously think about their intellectual framework. Unfortunately, this is not even an issue of debate in India.

The history of Delhi illustrates the impact of prevailing ideologies. What is now called Old Delhi was built by Mughal Emperor Shah Jahan in the seventeenth century. It was a city with grand palaces for the nobility, interspersed with the desperate hovels where the common people lived—reflecting the feudal hierarchy of that time. The hierarchy culminated in the Red Fort, where the emperor's family lived.

When the British built New Delhi, they placed an imposing Viceroy's Palace (now Rashtrapati Bhavan) at its centre to reflect imperial power. It was a city of broad avenues for grand parades and large bungalows for the chosen few. When the city expanded under socialist rule, it added large areas to house the rapidly expanding bureaucracy required in a State-run system. This led to 'planned' additions like Rama Krishna Puram—homes for civil servants with little space for commerce. Finally, when the economy was liberalised in the Nineties, we witnessed the explosive, if unregulated, growth of Gurgaon (now, Gurugram). It is a good reflection of today's India—a booming private sector, a government struggling to keep up and the whiff of the robber-baron.

As one can see, the intellectual underpinnings of each period are clearly reflected in how the city developed. Those who manage the world's great cities are aware of this. New York's buzz, London's cool quirkiness, and Singapore's smooth efficiency are the result of deliberate thought that gives the cities their personality.

The problem with Indian urban thinking is that it was captured in the twentieth century by Le Corbusier's idea that a building or a city is a 'machine for living'. The idea was that cities were mechanical systems with neat silos that could be managed by a central authority. This fitted both Corbusier's fascist leanings as well as Nehru's socialism. It is no coincidence that it contains the same mechanistic world view reflected in the economic plans of P.C. Mahalanobis.

Many cities were built in the Fifties and Sixties with this ideology, but not one has been a success. India's more successful cities are still of colonial origin. Even Chandigarh, the expensive poster child of Corbusier, has produced little of commercial or cultural value after half a century of existence. It remains a city of tax-consuming bureaucrats. What little vibrancy it has shown in recent years comes from the suburb of Mohali, which is outside Corbusier's plan.

So how should we think of our cities?

One of the common themes across all successful international cities is that they think of themselves as evolving ecosystems. In other words, the city is seen as a bubbling mix of people, ideas, public amenities, buildings, institutions and so on. Success is driven by the constant—and often unpredictable—interactions between these elements. The city is, therefore, more than the sum of its parts. Note the contrast with the mechanical world view of static 'master plans' and neatly-zoned silos that still dominate Indian urban thinking.

Let me illustrate how these different views lead to radically different outcomes. In the last few months, both Singapore and Delhi hosted Formula One races. Delhi created a custom-built race tract at the edge of the city at considerable expense, while Singapore held the event in the middle of its city. By using existing roads, Singapore avoided acquiring new land or building new infrastructure. Of course, special arrangements had to be made, but the price tag was small.

Yet, it was Singapore that gained more from the event. The spectacle of fast cars whizzing around its downtown created a big buzz—hotels, bars and restaurants were packed and its skyline was constantly beamed around the world for two days. Delhi's custom-built race track is arguably better for racing, but the city hardly benefitted from the event. Instead, it created expensive infrastructure that is used for two days in a year. Even worse, it is Singapore that will continue to host Formula One, while Delhi seems to have lost its slot.

The difference between the two cities is that Singapore saw Formula One as part of an overall effort to bring buzz to the city's ecosystem, while Delhi thought of it as an engineering problem for fast automobiles. Delhi's race track is better, but it missed the point. Imagine, instead, the visual impact on world television of fluorescent Formula One cars screaming down Rajpath at night. Not only would this require little investment, but we wouldn't need to spend money on 'Incredible India' advertisements.

The same compartmentalised, mechanical world view shows up in many other places. Take, for instance, the building of new universities. Almost invariably it involves the acquisition of large tracts of land—often hundreds of acres—that are then walled off from the rest of the city. Thus, Kanpur and Kharagpur benefit little from the existence of large Indian Institute of Technology (IIT) campuses in their midst. If our urban planners thought of cities as organic ecosystems, they would see that universities are important ways for a city to engage with young people and encourage the exchange of ideas. That is why all great cities have universities as an integral part of their landscape.

The obvious failure of Corbusier's machines has left a void that is yet to be filled by new thinking. At the very least, we need to begin thinking of our cities as 'complex, adaptive ecosystems'. As illustrated above, it will allow us to rethink our urban issues in fresh ways.

(This piece was originally published in *Business Standard*, December 2013)

# LIBERALISING INDIA'S URBAN THINKING

A quarter of a century ago, India threw off the shackles of Nehruvian socialism and embarked on economic liberalisation. Since 1991, socialist-era thinking has been steadily discarded in a growing number of areas such as foreign policy, but it remains firmly embedded in how Indian cities are planned. This is the ultimate source of dissonance between the cities we build and the cities that twenty-first century India aspires to.

It may come as a surprise to many readers that ideology plays an important role in how cities develop. The fact is that every city is a living embodiment of some philosophy. What is now called Old Delhi, for instance, was a reflection of the hierarchical feudal order prevailing in the seventeenth century when Emperor Shah Jahan built it. It was a city of grand palaces and miserable slums. French traveller François Bernier who visited the city just a few years after it was built, tells us, 'A man must be of the highest rank or live miserably.' At the top of the urban hierarchy was the Red Fort where the royal family lived.

When the British decided to build New Delhi a century ago, they conceived of it as a city of grand imperial parades and a racially coded hierarchy. The city's early plans marked the most spacious bungalows as 'fat white' and lesser dwellings as 'thin white' and 'thin black'. As no senior Indian officials were envisaged, the plans do not mark 'fat black'. At the pinnacle of this city was a palace for the Viceroy, now Rashtrapati Bhavan.

After Independence, Delhi became a city of civil servants brought in to run the socialist economy. Thus Delhi evolved into a bureaucratic ladder made up of housing rungs called C-I, C-II, D-I, D-II and so on. The ideal city was seen as a giant machine designed by 'wise' urban planners. They imposed rigid master plans that neatly zoned different urban activities and strictly controlled urban evolution. The similarity with P.C. Mahalanobis' economic planning is not a coincidence. They are both outcomes of the same Nehruvian thinking.

French architect Le Corbusier was the urban planning equivalent to Mahalanobis. Just as Mahalanobis saw the economy as a mechanical input-output model, Le Corbusier saw buildings as 'machines for living'. The 'wise' planner created a detailed master plan, and success was all about meticulously implementing it. Innovation was allowed only if planners approved it, otherwise it was looked on with suspicion. It was not about managing an evolving ecosystem.

A large number of cities and urban extensions were

built using Le Corbusier's thinking, but not one succeeded. After two generations of trying, Durgapur, Dispur and Navi Mumbai can hardly be called successes. Even Chandigarh, Le Corbusier's poster child, is really a subsidised housing colony for serving and retired civil servants. Despite the deployment of enormous resources by two state governments and the national government, Chandigarh has not produced anything of economic or cultural value. Whatever buzz it produces comes from the suburb of Mohali that is outside Corbusier's plan. Even Nek Chand's famous rock garden was built illegally.

Despite his obvious failures, Le Corbusier is still held in high esteem in India and his ideas are deeply embedded in urban codes. Any attempt to tamper with Chandigarh's plan is met with howls of protest. This is ironical because, in the rest of the world, his ideas were discredited long ago by the likes of Lewis Mumford and Jane Jacobs. With post-Independence planning stuck in a quagmire, twenty-first century India continues to rely on colonial-era urban codes. New cities such as Gurugram develop by ignoring official master plans.

So what should be done? The first step is to stop thinking of the city as a machine and start thinking of it as an evolving ecosystem. Thus, success is about flexibility and managing change rather than implementing brilliant master plans.

Indians often mistake Singapore's success as that of outstanding planning, but the reality is that the city-state is really a great example of flexibility and constant tinkering. Since it became independent in 1965, Singapore has gone from

British naval base to shipping and manufacturing cluster, then to financial centre and more recently to education and entertainment hub. Each step needed radical urban surgery. During the same period, Indians have faithfully preserved Chandigarh's original master plan.

Every fifteen years or so, Singapore completely re-evaluates its overall economic and urban strategy. The last time this happened was in 2002–03 in the aftermath of the Asian crisis. The rethink led to new university campuses, entertainment hubs, Formula One racing and so on. The government has just initiated a new round. It's all about new ideas, tinkering, feedback loops and managing transitions. Having personally participated in the process, it is eye-opening how fundamentally different this approach is from urban discussions in India.

A quarter century ago, India's economic thinking broke away from socialist planning. Now India's urban thinking needs liberalisation. Even if we did our very best on Chandigarh, the best we can hope for is Canberra or Brasilia. On the other hand, if we managed Gurugram better, we could get Singapore or Hong Kong.

(This piece was originally published in *Mint*, July 2016)

# REVIVING VARANASI FOR THE 21ST CENTURY

Despite its importance as a religious centre and tourist hub, anyone visiting Varanasi can see that it's a city crumbling from neglect. Therefore, one hopes that some good will come out of all the attention it has attracted during the election campaign of 2014. Whoever wins the contest will become an important national figure, and will presumably have the clout to make real changes. But what needs to be done?

Although I have never lived in Varanasi, I have visited it several times and feel a strong emotional connection with it. My family is of Bengali extraction, but it settled in Varanasi in the mid-eighteenth century. We continued to live there till the British colonial government confiscated our ancestral homes and drove us out in 1929 for participating in the freedom struggle. Many male members of the family went into hiding or were jailed, some never to return. Yet, I found many lingering reminders of my family in the winding lanes of Madanpura—including the Bengali Tola Inter-College, one of the first modern schools in north India, established in 1854 by my forefathers.

I have often asked town planners and local officials about what could be done to revive Varanasi. The answer usually is that not much can be done, because it's such an old city, with narrow winding lanes, that it is impossible to introduce any modern infrastructure. The best one can hope for is that we build planned extensions to the city with wide roads and modern amenities so that the old city can be 'decongested'— that is, it would be a great city if only we can introduce neat suburban houses and broad boulevards suitable for cars. Meanwhile, the old city is seen as a legacy problem to be kept somehow alive for tourists.

There is a problem with this framework of thinking. If the so-called improvements had actually been made, Varanasi would have been reduced by now to Navi Mumbai or Delhi's Dwarka, soulless products of a twentieth-century 'modernism' that has been discarded everywhere except in India. So how should we think of Varanasi in the twenty-first century?

Today's leading urban thinkers no longer advocate cities as machines that must be run to a 'master plan' that maximises efficiency. Instead, cities are seen as evolving ecosystems that organically mix and match many ingredients. Thus, a successful city is one that encourages human interaction, has accessible public spaces, conserves historical heritage, is conducive to walking, creates human capital/diversity and, horror of horrors, mixes commercial and residential uses.

When seen from this lens, the urban design of Varanasi no longer seems a problem. The narrow winding lanes and their idiosyncratic twists are a nightmare for cars, but make perfect sense on foot. High density, mixed use and distinct neighbourhoods create urban buzz and encourage human interaction. The *ghats* provide public spaces open to all strata of society and actively utilises the riverfront, something most modern Indian cities fail to do. The multiple layers of history, the organic mix of halwai shops, temples and homes, and the bubbling mix of people from different backgrounds give Varanasi a personality that would otherwise be impossible to create by deliberate design.

Moreover, the urban cluster is more than just the old city strung along the ghats. For instance, the city is also home to numerous educational institutions, including the Banaras Hindu University (BHU), one of India's top universities and the largest residential university in Asia. The city is also at the heart of India's transportation network. Ancient India had two major highways—the Uttarapath, or northern road, and the Dakshinapath, or southern road. These highways met just outside Varanasi at Sarnath. Incredibly, two of India's most important highways still meet at Varanasi: NH2, which roughly follows the old Uttarapath, and NH7, which runs all the way down to Kanyakumari. A short distance away is Mughalsarai (now Pt. Deendayal Upadhyaya Junction), the nerve centre of the country's railway network.

As one can see, Varanasi already enjoys most of the elements required for a successful urban ecosystem. The problem is not its urban design and, consequently, the solution is not better 'planning', but better 'management'. There is a big difference between these two approaches.

The management approach to Varanasi would emphasise the following. First, the single most important thing would be to clean up the city. For the most part, this is about better management of existing municipal services—garbage clearance, drainage, controlling stray animals and so on.

Second, the surrounding river system needs to be revived. People usually pay attention only to the Ganga, but the city has other rivers. In fact, its very name is derived from the Varuna and the Asi rivers. The Varuna is still a discernable stream, but the Asi has been reduced to a sewage-filled drain. Many locals who live next to the Asi were surprised when I told them that they lived along its banks.

Third, the city's intellectual cluster needs to be enhanced. The current fashion is to build new universities in sprawling campuses in remote locations. But this disperses intellectual clusters. It is far better to enhance existing hubs like Varanasi. This will need investment in new institutions, conference facilities, laboratories within a short distance of the city, and a deliberate effort to encourage the exchange of ideas.

Fourth, large parts of the old city should be pedestrianised. Some motorable roads can be left in place for emergencies and for bringing in supplies; but a clean, safe walking network would transform the feel of the city, as happened in the medieval city centres of Europe. Perhaps an elevated monorail could be built to run parallel to the river at a distance of half a kilometre inland so that locals and visitors can go about their business by combining walking with a reliable public transport backbone.

Finally, the city's historical heritage is crumbling and needs urgent investment. It is not merely the passage of time; in many cases, there is thoughtless defacement from advertising hoardings and unauthorised construction. As the reader will recognise, the approach of 'managing' Varanasi organically and adding to its ecosystem is fundamentally different from the approach of adding 'planned' sectors and widening roads.

Looking at Varanasi from a post-modernist lens resolves one of the great mysteries of Indian history—why did ancient Indians not build rigidly planned cities after the Bronze Age?

It is now known that the Harappan cities were abandoned around 2000 BC due to climate change and the drying of the Saraswati river (and not marauding central Asians). Some of the refugees moved east to the Gangetic plains where they built great Iron Age cities, but historians have perpetuated the idea that these cities were somehow inferior to the Harappan cities. From a post-modernist view, however, the Iron Age cities were just as successful as the urban centres. Indeed, the great Harappan cities were abandoned after just a few hundred years, whereas the Iron Age city of Varanasi has survived more than three thousand years and, perhaps with a bit of care, may survive another three thousand.

*Note: Recent studies suggest that Varanasi may be a lot older than previously believed and a settlement may have existed here in the Bronze Age—this only strengthens the case made in the essay.

(This piece was originally published in *Business Standard*, May 2014)

# BUILDING BOSTONS, NOT KANPURS

Around the world, universities are the stuff that makes great cities. Imagine Boston without Harvard, MIT and the myriad other institutions that are clustered around the Boston–Cambridge area. In Britain, Oxford and Cambridge are vibrant urban centres that derive their vigour almost entirely from playing host to famous universities. Even large and diversified global cities like London and New York would be much diminished without the intellectual clustering of LSE, Columbia, UCL and NYU. In each case, the universities are an integral part of the urban landscape and are consciously leveraged by their host cities.

Yet, Indian cities do not think of their universities and research institutes as important drivers of urban growth. At most, they are seen as utilitarian places for teaching students. Their importance for clustering human capital and driving innovation is simply not seen as part of the overall urban strategy. Indeed, universities built after Independence have been sealed off on campuses, often in distant locations, that deliberately discourage interaction with the wider city. Thus, Kanpur and Kharagpur benefit little from being host to a prestigious institution like the IIT. This is absurd.

## THE SOFTWARE OF CITIES

Urban development is not just about the 'hardware'— buildings, roads, plumbing and so on. It is the people, their social/economic activity and their continuous interaction that bring cities alive. Successful cities are those that can cluster human capital and encourage innovation, creativity and exchange of ideas. This has always been true. Think of the great cities of the past: Athens, Rome, Constantinople, Alexandria, Ujjain and Varanasi. However, this factor has become even more important in the twenty-first century. Never before has the economic value of ideation and creativity been greater. In short, the 'software' is critical to the evolution of a city.

Universities are key to the software of a city. They attract young talent, encourage the churn of ideas and trigger innovation. The physical infrastructure of the university provides the venue for conferences, seminars and cultural/ sporting events that allow for intense human interaction. Note how NYU played an important role in regenerating Lower Manhattan in the Nineties.

Next generation global cities like Singapore recognise this dynamic and use it actively as part of urban/national economic strategy. For instance, Singapore has built out a number of new institutions like the Singapore Management

University over the last decade. In most cases, these have been clustered in the middle of the city rather than on remote campuses. The city benefits from having a throughput of young people in the city-centre. At the same time, the university benefits from easy access to industry, government and urban buzz.

Prior to Independence, the role of universities in urban areas was appreciated. The colleges of Bombay, and Calcutta were built into the city much like the colleges of London. Banaras Hindu University and Delhi University, although built as a separate campus, was still seen as a part of the overall urban fabric. There were even important towns like Allahabad and Aligarh that were driven largely by their vibrant universities, much like Oxford and Cambridge.

Contrast this to how tertiary education institutions were built after Independence. All the IITs and IIMs are large, sealed campuses built originally outside the city. The model was the industrial-era factory township.

The physical walls that surround them have continued to wall them off socially and intellectually from their host cities even where urban growth has brought them inside the city. How different are they from the urban campuses of MIT and Harvard Business School. This is a loss to both sides.

## PERPETUATING THE MISTAKE

We appear to have learned little from our past. Indeed, this is not even considered an issue worthy of attention and debate. Thus, the establishment of a new university or institute is still about acquiring large tracts of land, often hundreds of acres, and then constructing stand-alone buildings. If anything, success is measured by how much land has been acquired rather than the quality of education/research.

This is a very wasteful process at many levels. First, it is unnecessarily converting productive farm and forest land. Why does Vedanta need 6,000 acres in Odisha and IIT Jodhpur 700 acres in Rajasthan for teaching a few thousand students?

Second, it requires the creation of expensive infrastructure in isolated locations, including staff housing, convocation halls, seminar rooms and so on. How many times a year is the convocation hall used by the institution itself? In a location within the city, these facilities would have added to the overall urban infrastructure.

Third, such remote campuses are inconsiderate of the social, educational and career needs of the families of the faculty and staff. This is a major constraint to finding good faculty. We cannot build universities as if they are industrial-era factory townships where the wives stay at home and the children study in the company school.

Finally, and most damagingly, these campuses are unable to generate the externalities that one would associate with a good academic/research institute. Students come and leave. There is no clustering or inter-linkage with the real world.

The proposed IIT in Jodhpur is an example of how we are perpetuating the flawed model. The government has already acquired 700 acres of land about twenty-two kms from Jodhpur. There's a lot of talk about how it will be a green campus with solar panels and electric buses ferrying people from the city/airport. A number of complex options are being discussed to supply it with water. This is all meaningless when the most energy-efficient solution would have been to have a compact campus that is closer to the city. This would have automatically reduced the need to travel long distances and recreate social infrastructure. In addition, Jodhpur city has a problem with rising water tables and there is absolutely no need for expensive water-supply technologies when it can simply be pumped out. Worst of all, given the distance, the existing city will gain nothing from the building of all this expensive infrastructure.

To conclude, universities are an important part of the urban economy and should be seen as an integral part of city-building. As we build out new institutions, we urgently need to stop thinking of them as fenced-off factory townships. We do not need more Kanpurs and Kharagpurs. If India wants to play on the global stage, it needs to create its very own Bostons and Oxfords.

(This piece was originally published in *Business Standard*, May 2010)

# MUMBAI NEEDS AN ICONIC MUSEUM

Cities are in vogue these days with talk of smart cities and of turning Mumbai into an international financial centre. Unfortunately, most of the discussion centres on the hardware: buildings, flyovers, monorail....Urban hardware is indeed important. But great cities like Mumbai also need world-class 'software'. Look at any great city and one will see it's not just about glass and chrome office buildings and swish airports, but also about social interaction, economic activity, culture, entertainment and urban buzz.

So, the debate about the future of Indian cities must not be limited to functional civil engineering, but extended to things that bring a city to life. It is extraordinary that a proud civilisation like India has hardly built a world-class purpose-built museum since Independence. Yet, we would have happily paid to see the Metropolitan Museum of Art (the MET) in New York, the Victoria and Albert Museum in London and the Louvre in Paris, and gawked at the displays of Indian artifacts, when similar artifacts lie forgotten all over India.

This is not about sentimentality. Great museums are an important 'soft' ingredient of a metropolis and can have real economic value. The Louvre, for instance, welcomed 9.3 million visitors in 2013, the MET 6.8 million, while the British Museum had 6.7 million visitors. Museums in the US employ 4,00,000 people and directly contribute twenty-one billion dollars to the nation's economy. Indeed, cities like Bilbao have anchored their revival on the back of a great museum. This is why there is a case for building an iconic maritime museum in Mumbai.

But why a maritime museum? Indian history textbooks give the impression that the country's past is all about land-based empires. But Indian civilisation has always had a huge maritime footprint. After all, it is the only country that has an ocean named after it.

There is evidence that the Harappans were trading with Mesopotamia 4,500 years ago. After the collapse of the Harappan civilisation, 'Indians' continued to explore the Indian Ocean. By the sixth century BC, merchants from Odisha were sailing along the eastern coast of India and were settling in Sri Lanka in large numbers.

This is why the Sinhalese majority of Sri Lanka is of Odiya–Bengali origin and speaks a related language.

By the third century BC, Indian merchants were confident enough to sail across the Indian Ocean to Southeast Asia. This trade led to the spread of Indic culture to this part of the world and we see the rise of Hindu–Buddhist kingdoms in Java, Sumatra, Cambodia and Vietnam. By the second century BC, we also saw flourishing trade relations with the Greeks and later the Roman empire. Eventually, Indian seafarers and merchants would create a maritime network that stretched from China in the east to Iraq and Alexandria in the west.

Although Indian maritime activity was mostly about peaceful trade, some Indian kingdoms did project naval power. The best-known examples are the naval raids by the Cholas on the Srivijaya kingdom of Sumatra in eleventh century. In the eighteenth century, the Maratha navy led by Admiral Kanhoji Angre gave the British and Portuguese a hard time.

All this maritime activity had a profound impact. Syrian Christians, Arabs, Parsis and Jews came to India as traders and refugees, and brought their cultures with them, just as Indian merchants spread Hinduism and Buddhism to Southeast Asia and beyond. The second-oldest mosque in the world is in Kerala, quite close to some of the oldest apostolic churches in the world, while the largest Hindu temple ever built, Angkor Wat, is in Cambodia.

Even Indian cuisine has been profoundly influenced by spices brought from Indonesia; vegetables such as tomatoes and potatoes were introduced by the Portuguese; while there were other and assorted Arab and Persian influences. A maritime museum is a great way to celebrate this history of our globalisation and trade, and the extraordinary diversity created by the cross-pollination of ideas, food, religions, literature and, as a consequence, cultures.

Mumbai is the obvious location for it, given its strong maritime traditions. The problem in a crowded city is to find real estate to match the ambition of such a project. Fortunately, there are plans to redevelop 1,800 acres of Port Trust land spread across the city's eastern seaboard. Much of it will go towards offices, residential buildings and open areas. However, there is a case for using a maritime museum as a key anchor tenant to create a cultural hub that serves not just as a reminder of our glorious maritime past, but also one that has theatres, lecture halls, restaurants and other amenities that contribute to a vibrant urban environment.

Ideally, it must be an iconic waterfront building that adds to the city's skyline, like the Sydney Opera House or the Bund in Shanghai. How long will Mumbai's architectural personality depend on the colonial era? As the commercial capital of a rising twenty-first century power, it must recast its image in a way that both captures our past and points the way to our future, and becomes by itself one of the key reasons for people to visit the city.

Our hope is that government, business, civil society, academia and others will get behind this effort to enable us to tell our own history. In Mumbai. On the waterfront.

(This article was first published in *The Economic Times*, April 2015, and is credited to the author and Reuben Abraham).

# REIGNITING KOLKATA'S SPIRIT

At the beginning of the twentieth century, Calcutta (as it was known then) was the capital of the British Empire in India and its writ ran large from the Khyber Pass to Burma (now Myanmar). It was arguably the most advanced and cosmopolitan city in Asia. Its streets bustled with people from all over India and the world including, Marwaris, Jews, Armenians, Europeans, and of course local Bengalis. It even had a vibrant Chinatown! It was home to Swami Vivekananda, Subhas Bose, Rabindranath Tagore to name a few who built modern India.

Even after the capital shifted to New Delhi and later, during post-Partition, the city remained the cultural, intellectual and economic heart of India. In 1950, Calcutta's metropolitan area had a population of 4.5 million compared to Bombay's 2.9 million and Delhi's 1.4 million. Many of the country's top companies were headquartered in the city and its industrial cluster was the largest in Asia outside of Japan. Yet, today's Kolkata rarely merits a mention for its economic or even cultural achievements. In the late Sixties, it ceded its position as India's commercial capital to Mumbai and has made no effort to regain it. It remains the country's third largest metropolitan region after Mumbai and Delhi, but in terms of economic importance it lags behind Bengaluru, Hyderabad, Chennai and perhaps even Pune and Ahmedabad. What went wrong? Can Kolkata's spirit be re-ignited?

Kolkata suffers from many of the same problems that plague other Indian cities ranging from traffic jams to slums. However, it would be difficult to argue that Kolkata's physical infrastructure is especially bad. Water and power supply is far more erratic in Delhi, the traffic jams are far worse in Bengaluru and the public transport system is far more crowded in Mumbai. Yet, Kolkata has lagged far behind all these cities. The reason is that Kolkata's problems stem from its software rather than its hardware.

Urban software relates to social, economic, cultural and intellectual activities that animate a city and give it life. In particular, it relates to the clustering of human capital. Till the 1960s, Calcutta had the best clustering of human capital in India, including industrial workers, corporate managers, artists and scholars. This human capital cluster unwound in the late Sixties and Seventies and completely disintegrated in the Eighties.

This was the consequence of a cultural and political milieu that actively discouraged innovation and risk-taking of any kind. The impact of aggressive trade unionism on Kolkata's commercial sector is well known. Less known is the impact of cultural close-mindedness on intellectual innovation. The teaching of English was stopped in government-run primary schools. Heterodox intellectuals like Nirad Chaudhury were actively persecuted. Institutions like Calcutta University were deemed elitist and either ignored or deliberately subverted. For half a century, there was a ban on any form of innovation in the way Tagore's works were performed. His songs and plays had to be performed according to strict formulae. The result was that Kolkata went from being a cosmopolitan city to becoming a provincial town. Not surprisingly, the city's once proud middle-class scattered all over India and the world.

The city's economic dynamism left with them; I know this from personal experience as only few of my childhood friends and classmates still live in the city. Kolkatans may be proud of Prof Amartya Sen, Shashi Tharoor and Laxmi Mittal, but these successful individuals left the city decades ago.

In recent years, the citizens and those who govern Kolkata have begun to recognise the need for change. As readers will know, the initial efforts at reviving the industrial sector have got tied down by disputes over land acquisition. However, the real issue is not the availability of industrial land or urban hardware. The real problem is that the city's software needs to be upgraded and the human capital cluster needs to be rebuilt.

In one of my pieces, I had argued that urban re-engineering should rely less on master plans and more on strategic interventions. Usually, these strategic investments relate to hardware such as the Delhi Metro. However, in Kolkata's case the required strategic interventions involve investing in software.

Kolkata is still home to a disproportionately large number of cultural and intellectual institutions, many of them built during the British rule. These include academic institutions like Calcutta University (and famous colleges like Presidency and St. Xavier's), the Indian Statistical Institute and the Indian Institute of Management at Joka. Not far away are IIT-Kharagpur and Viswa Bharati, Shantiniketan. Kolkata is also home to the National Library, the Asiatic Society and to the Indian Museum, Asia's oldest museum. Kolkata still holds one of the world's largest book fairs and possibly the most spectacular religious carnival—the Durga Puja (sorry, Rio). It even has the world's most extraordinary collection of colonial-era buildings including architectural treasures like the Victoria Memorial and Writer's Building.

All of these are assets of enormous economic value. The future of Kolkata lies in unlocking this value. Unfortunately, virtually all of these assets have been allowed to decay for decades. The city's government, its citizens and its well-wishers need to re-invest in them and revive Kolkata as a hub of cultural/intellectual innovation. This is not an elitist vision about high-culture but one that goes to the heart of what gives a great city its buzz. Cities like New York, London and even Mumbai are not just great commercial hubs but also important cultural and intellectual hubs. Their secret of success is the bubbling cauldron of ideas and influences (Raj Thackarey should learn to appreciate this).

To conclude, Kolkata's revival needs investment in its software rather than in its hardware. We need to re-ignite the spirit that animated the city in the nineteenth and early twentieth centuries. This needs investment of money and effort in bringing back its cultural and intellectual institutions (and building a few new ones as well). In turn, this will build back the cluster of human capital that once drove the economy. And best of all, this strategy does not require large-scale land acquisitions!

(This piece was originally published in *Business Standard*, January 2013)

# THE EYES ON THE STREET

Urban crimes, particularly those directed at women, have been a cause of growing outrage in India over the last couple of years. Given the frequency and nature of some of these crimes, the outrage is entirely justified. But why are we witnessing such a sharp increase in crimes against women? Self-styled social activists and intellectuals love to rant on television about outdated socio-cultural mores and traditional patriarchal attitudes. However, there is reason to believe that such factors play no more than a small role in feeding this growing problem.

Take, for example, Kolkata, a city that was once famed for being safe for women. I have personally witnessed how it has steadily become less safe for women since the early 1980s. Is this because Bengalis have suddenly become more patriarchal? Indeed, there is no evidence that crimes against women are greater in the more traditional Indian cities like Madurai, Udaipur, Ahmedabad, Surat or Thiruvananthapuram.

Instead, the increase in crime is being reported from the more modern cities like Delhi's National Capital Region (NCR) and Mumbai. Even within Delhi, it is remarkable that all the high-profile incidents occurred in the newer parts of the city and not in traditionalist Old Delhi. Clearly, 'traditional attitudes' is not the full story. One can even make the opposite case in some parts of the country. Guwahati has seen a rise in crimes against women in recent years, including a televised mob lynching. Yet, women have traditionally enjoyed high social status in Assam and other north-eastern states. The recent trend, if anything, is a deviation from traditional values.

Violent urban crime, including those targeted at women, are not unique to India. Cities in the United States witnessed a sharp deterioration between the 1960s and 1990s. Jane Jacobs, one of the greatest urban thinkers of the twentieth century, closely observed this period of urban collapse and concluded that the key factor that kept cities safe was 'eyes on the street'—the fact that people were watching.

Note that 'eyes on the street' is not about having a crowd. A road with heavy traffic may have a lot of people, but they are merely passing through and not engaging with their surroundings. In contrast, a street vendor or an old retiree on a park bench is likely to be observing what is going on.

In the Indian context, the 'eyes on the street' were traditionally provided by the ecosystem of the *nukkad*, or street corner—the local barber, the grocery shop, the paanwala, the chaiwala, the nosey neighbour and so on. This general model has many variants ranging from the *pol* in Ahmedabad to the *para* or locality in Kolkata.

The problem is that modern urban planning has completely disregarded this software aspect of the city. In the pursuit of a false aesthetic ideal, planners segregated the multiple activities that give life to urban ecosystems. Commerce and street life were deliberately zoned away from where people lived, thereby leaving few spaces for informal social interaction.

So, when Kolkata expanded into Salt Lake and then more recently into Rajarhat, the para did not follow since the so-called planning made no provision for the locals to gather together for the evening *adda* at the 'rock'. Not surprisingly, the newer areas remain more crime-prone than the old city. We find the same phenomenon in other parts of the world. It is no coincidence that the hopelessly crime-ridden banlieues of Paris were built using the ideas of the same Le Corbusier who continues to dominate Indian urban thinking.

The second important ingredient for a safe city is visible governance. Routine rule-breaking is a fact of life in India. Most of the time, it involves nothing more than giving small bribes or breaking traffic rules, but a visible lack of governance attracts further rule-breaking. The most commonly quoted illustration of this point is the 'broken window theory'. As numerous studies have shown, if you leave a car or a house with a broken window, it soon attracts others to completely vandalise it.

The most famous application of the broken window theory was mayor Rudy Giuliani's crackdown on petty crimes in New York in the 1990s. During the following decade, crime rates dropped dramatically—although some commentators argue that other factors may have also played a role. In India's case, however, there is a general sense that the system is simply unable or unwilling to punish the guilty for big crimes or small. Even terrorists can escape punishment if it is politically convenient. Thus, the rise in rapes is closely related to the increase in crimes ranging from large-scale corruption to violent road rage.

In Kautilya's *Arthashastra,* this situation is called *matsya nyaya,* or Law of the Fish (in other words, the big fish eat the small). That is why Kautilya argues that the rule of law is the single most important responsibility of the State. As certain recent events have illustrated, no amount of public espousing of 'modern' or 'liberal' values can substitute for the legal system when it comes to ensuring justice for women.

The good news is that once governance has been established in an urban ecosystem, it requires relatively little overt action to sustain it. In the 1970s, Singapore cracked down severely on criminal gangs but also introduced steep fines on petty things such as spitting and littering. Today, a visitor to Singapore may go for weeks without even spotting a policeman (unlike in an Indian city). I have also never met anyone who has been fined for littering, but the overall sense of governance remains.

To conclude, the blaming of violent crimes against women

merely on socio-cultural values may serve the ideological agendas of some people, but it is diverting attention from the real business of solving the problem. As discussed in this piece, urban design and the rule of law must be an important part of the solution.

(This piece was originally published in *Business Standard*, March 2014)

# WHY INDIA NEEDS TO SLUM IT OUT

Indian policymakers have at last accepted that urbanisation is an essential part of economic development. Indeed, current trends suggest that India will be an urban-majority country by 2040. If Prime Minister Narendra Modi succeeds in implementing his plan for rapid industrialisation, the country would hit the milestone even sooner. The implication of this shift is that 300-350 million additional people will have to be accommodated in urban centres within a generation. The prime minister clearly appreciates the issue and his plan to create a hundred smart cities should be seen as an attempt to create urban infrastructure in anticipation of the deluge.

While it is good that policymakers are paying more attention to cities, it is important to recognise that urbanisation is a dynamic process. In particular, we need to think about how millions of people will get matched to jobs, homes and amenities, according to their needs and abilities. India's predicament was faced by today's developed countries when they urbanised in the nineteenth and early twentieth centuries. So what was the mechanism that sucked in millions of people and slotted them into the urban landscape of Europe, North America and Japan? The answer: slums.

Most people think of slums as places of static despair as depicted in films such as *Slumdog Millionaire*—the only way out is to win a lottery. While the poverty is real enough, real-life slums could not be more different. If one looks past the open drains and plastic sheets, one will see that slums are ecosystems buzzing with activity—shops, mini-factories, people moving in, people moving out. This is where migrants will first find shelter, get their first job, get connected with social networks and get information about opportunities in the wider city.

Almost every country has had slums during the urbanisation phase. The slums of London and New York were notorious well into the twentieth century. A century ago, the now trendy Meatpacking District of Manhattan had more than 200 slaughterhouses where many immigrants worked so that their children could move to the leafy suburbs. Harappan cities and Mughal Delhi also had slums. Even today's China has slums, despite its many social and political controls including the Hukou permit system. Slums already play a critical role as routers in India's migration process. According to estimates by UN-Habitat, sixty million people moved 'out' of Indian slums between 2000 and 2010.

Some may have gone back home, but many climbed the economic ladder into the new urban middle class. This is exactly why slums continue to attract new migrants despite the awful living conditions—migrants know that they, or at least their children, have a fighting chance of breaking out of the cycle of poverty. Understanding urban poverty as a dynamic flow has very important implications about how we design and manage future cities. First, we need to design for urban spaces that will play the role of slums. This is not about solving a housing problem but the functioning of a wider ecosystem. Thus, creating neat low-income housing estates will not work unless they allow for many of the messy economic and social activities that thrive in slums. By building it into the design, 'smart slums' can support the migration process while mitigating the squalor.

Second, property rights have to be arranged so that new migrants can enter the system easily and climb the socio-economic ladder. This would include cheap rental accommodation, easy financing to allow home purchase, liquid secondary markets and so on. This is very different from the current thinking that emphasises subsidised housing for the poor, but then gives non-marketable ownership rights. From a flow perspective, the subsidy is less important than the availability of alternatives, ease of entry, clear property rights, financing and a secondary market that allow new migrants to climb the ladder.

Third, access to the 'commons' is very important to the lives of the poor. The lowest rung in the housing ladder can be fairly basic, including dormitories, but must ensure access to public transport, schools, sanitation, security and social networks.

To conclude, slums have always played an important role in the urbanisation process. This is where new migrants are absorbed and naturalised into the urban system. Indian policy-makers need to design for urban spaces that will play the same role in the new smart cities. By anticipating this need, one hopes that the absorption process can be made more efficient and the worst of the squalor can be avoided.

(This piece was originally published in *India Today*, September 2014)

# HOW TO SEED SMART CITIES

In his Budget speech, Arun Jaitley reiterated the NDA government's plan to build a hundred 'smart cities', presumably by upgrading and expanding existing towns and perhaps raising a few new urban centres. The finance minister also announced five new IITs, as many IIMs and four AIIMS-pattern institutions. Fine proposals, except that these will be seen as separate, mutually exclusive projects during implementation. That would be a pity, for these are inextricably linked. Universities, for instance, are critical to making cities successful. It is almost impossible to imagine Boston, without Harvard, MIT and other institutions clustered in and around the Boston–Cambridge area. In Britain, Oxford and Cambridge are vibrant towns largely because they host the two famous universities. Indeed, many global cities such as London and New York would be much diminished without LSE, LBS, Columbia University, NYU. Rather than being walled off from the rest of the two cities, these institutions are an integral part of their urban ecosystems.

Newly successful cities such as Singapore too have invested heavily in universities, think tanks and research institutes, not just as centres for intellectual activity but as part of the wider urban ecosystem. Indeed, when the country's government planned the Singapore Management University, it set it up in the middle of the city. The city benefits from the urban buzz brought by young people while the university profits from being close to State and corporate institutions. Contrast this with Indian planners' idea of academic institutions as merely places for teaching students that have little direct link with the daily functioning of the city. This is so because they see town projects as mechanical silos and do not think in terms of organic ecosystems. Thus, universities built after Independence were housed in sealed-off campuses, often in remote places, that discourage interaction with the city.

Modelled on a socialist-era factory township, their walls continue to isolate them socially and intellectually even where the cities have expanded to surround them. This is why Kanpur and Kharagpur benefit little from being home to a prestigious institution like an IIT. Even in Delhi and Mumbai, IITs are closed worlds. Before Independence, on the other hand, universities were seen as part of the urban fabric. The colleges of Bombay and Calcutta were built into the city much like those of London. Allahabad and Aligarh were driven largely by their vibrant universities, much like Oxford and Cambridge.

Whenever I ask Indian officials and planners about 'smart cities', I get a laundry list of hardware infrastructure that is needed: state-of-the-art public transportation, smart power grids and so on. This is indeed important, but it overlooks the fact that cities are ultimately about people, not buildings. Successful cities are those that can cluster human capital and encourage innovation, creativity and exchange of ideas. To be 'smart' therefore, cities need both hardware and software. Universities are an essential part of this software. This is why great cities of the past—Athens, Florence, Constantinople, Rome, Alexandria, Ujjain, Varanasi—were almost always also great intellectual centres. They attracted talent, encouraged the churn of ideas and triggered innovation. Translated in modern terms, universities do not just attract young people to cities but provide venues for conferences, seminars, cultural and sporting events enabling human interaction that makes for lively urban clusters.

Now that the government has announced its intention to build new academic institutes, the focus will likely be on getting large tracts of land and constructing standalone buildings. If anything, success will be measured by how much land has been acquired. This is wasteful, and not just at one level. First, this approach requires unnecessary acquisition of productive farm and forest land. Why do we need hundreds of acres to educate a few thousand students? As Finance Minister Jaitley would know, his alma mater, Shri Ram College of Commerce, runs one of India's top colleges on just seventeen acres. There are many top-notch institutions around the world that operate from much less.

Second, a standalone institute requires the creation of expensive infrastructure in isolated locations, including staff housing, convocation halls, seminar rooms and so on. But how often will the convocation hall be used? In a city location, these facilities would have added to the overall urban infrastructure. Moreover, such remote campuses are inconsiderate of the social and career needs of the families of the faculty and staff, a major constraint to finding good faculty.

Finally, and most damagingly from an urban perspective, these isolated campuses are unable to add to the ecosystem. Students come and they leave, so human capital does not accumulate in the host city. Contrast this with the innovation clusters of Boston or Cambridge, UK.

The government should, therefore, consider using new institutions to seed 'smart cities'. This would mean weaving new IITs, IIMs and AIIMSs into the surrounding urban fabric. This may look messy on a master plan drawing board but, on the ground, it would create cities that are vibrant and, indeed, smart.

(This piece was originally published in *India Today*, July 2014)

# IN DEFENSE OF GURUGRAM

Fascists and socialists have one thing in common—the urge to impose rigid master plans on cities. In 1950, Prime Minister Jawaharlal Nehru invited Le Corbusier to design the new city of Chandigarh. Corbusier was specifically asked by Nehru to create a city that was unfettered by India's ancient civilisation. Enormous resources in land, material and money were poured into building the new city. At the same, rigid master plans were imposed on existing cities. Delhi was master planned in 1962 into strict zones according to use. However, the static master plan is to the city what socialist planning is to the economy. Both cities and economies are organic and rapidly evolving eco-systems. Just like the Mahalonobis model of central planning damaged the Indian economy, the country's urban thinking was severely damaged by Le Corbusier's philosophy that buildings were machines for living.

This mechanical world view is echoed in the Delhi master plan of 1962, which proclaimed that 'there is undesirable mixing of land-uses almost everywhere in the city.' Just as the government had the right to control the economy through licenses, it also had the right to tell people where to live and where to work. The problem is that such an approach cannot create a living eco-system. New industrial cities such as Durgapur never took off and today's successful cities are still those with British-era roots.

Even Chandigarh, the expensive poster child of socialist-era master planning, has generated little of economic or cultural value after more than half a century of existence. Much of its apparent cleanliness comes from simply having left no space for the poor. Its apparent greenery creates a false sense of being environment-friendly but is mostly a result of gobbling a lot of land per capita. It remains a sterile and heavily subsidised city of tax-consuming bureaucrats that encourages neither entrepreneurship nor tax-generating jobs. This is particularly glaring given that it is the pampered capital of two prosperous states. Nehru had wanted Chandigarh to be the symbol of India's future. Instead, the face of twenty-first century India is a city that is chaotic, unplanned, infuriating, but undeniably dynamic: Gurugram (or Gurgaon, as it is still popularly known as).

## A HISTORY OF GURUGRAM

Gurugram lies to the south of Delhi and, according to legend, is said to have been the village of Dronacharya who taught martial arts to the cousins, Pandavas and Kauravas in the Mahabharata. Indeed, the names Gurugram and Gurgaon both literally mean the 'village of the teacher'. Despite its proximity to Delhi, however, the settlement of Gurugram was never particularly large. Its population was estimated at a mere 3,990 in 1881 and nearby towns like Rewari and Farrukhnagar had much larger populations. The Gazetteer of 1883-84 tells that the British used Gurgaon as a district headquarters and that the town consisted of a small market (Sadar Bazaar), public offices, dwellings of European residents and a settlement called Jacobpura named after a former Deputy Commissioner. An old road connected Gurgaon to Delhi via Mehrauli. The road roughly survives as the arterial M.G. Road but the contours of British-era settlement can just about be discerned if one goes to the busy marketplace in Old Gurgaon called Mahavir Chowk. One will also see the remains of an old serai used by caravans heading to/from Delhi. A few colonial era bungalows too survive.

For the first few decades after Independence, Gurgaon remained a relatively small town in a largely rural district. The first major change came when Sanjay Gandhi, son of the then Prime Minister Indira Gandhi, acquired a large plot of land to start an automobile company in the early 1970s. This is now the Maruti-Suzuki factory, but the project was not initially successful. From the early 1980s, however, a number of real estate developers, particularly DLF, began to acquire farmland along the Delhi border. The idea at this stage was to build a mostly low-rise suburbia for Delhi's retiring civil servants. Although the Maruti car factory did get going by 1983, no one really envisaged the town as an independent growth engine.

## LAISSEZ-FAIRE CITY

The whole dynamics changed after India liberalised its economy in 1991. This coincided with the communications and information technology revolutions. As India globalised, a number of multinational companies discovered that call centres and back-office operations could be outsourced to India. Delhi was a good location for this because of available human capital and a well-connected international airport. However, the necessary real estate could not be created because of Delhi's rigid master plan. The old planners had never envisioned white-collar factories. The outsourcing companies, therefore, jumped across the border to Gurugram and began to build huge facilities for this new industry. This attracted young workers to the city and, in turn, encouraged the construction of malls and restaurants. As more corporate executives moved in, the retirement suburb format was abandoned in favour of condominiums. Schools and other educational institutions began to multiply. The pace of expansion can be gauged from a lone milestone that survives on M.G. Road under the elevated metro line (in front of Bristol Hotel). This is now the effective city centre but the milestone still proclaims that Gurugram is 6 km away.

The construction of Gurugram was not planned although a plan did exist in theory. It was made possible by a combination of a lack of rules and the blatant disregard of rules. There was always a whiff of the robber baron. Yet, what was a sleepy small town till the mid-1990s has become a throbbing city of gleaming office towers, metro stations, malls, luxury hotels and millions of jobs. With a population of over 3.5 million, it is no longer a mere suburb of Delhi but a city in its own right.

I am not suggesting that Gurugram does not have serious civic problems ranging from clogged roads and erratic power supply to the doings of unscrupulous property developers. I have more than enough personal experience of all these issues. It is true that with a little imagination and foresight, Gurugram could have been done a lot better. Nonetheless, it is hard to deny the bursting energy of the city. It is a good metaphor for modern India with its private sector dynamism, the robber baron element and a government that is struggling to keep up. Note that Gurugram single-handedly generates almost half of the revenues of the state of Haryana and it is this money that partly pays for Chandigarh. Meanwhile, if Chandigarh ever makes it as a successful city, it will be due to the dynamism of the suburb of Mohali and not the fascism of Corbusier.

(This piece was originally published in *Business Standard*, March 2011)

# OF DEAD RIVERS AND STRANDED ELEPHANTS

All discussions about urbanisation in India tend to focus on mega-cities like Mumbai, Delhi and Bengaluru. However, in states like Tamil Nadu and Gujarat, smaller urban centres are also seeing rapid growth. At one level, this is a good thing because it spreads economic activity and reduces pressure on the big cities. However, we need to be extra-sensitive when such disaggregated urban expansion occurs near ecologically vulnerable areas like the Nilgiris. The growth of the urban network around Coimbatore is an illustration of the dangers of expansion without proper regulation. It raises broader questions about how we manage our 'commons'.

## HISTORICAL BACKGROUND

Coimbatore is today an industrial town in the shadow of the Nilgiri mountains with a population of over 1.5 million.

However, a settlement on the banks of the Noyyal river has existed for almost two thousand years and was part of the trade route through the Palghat (or Pallakad) Gap. In the late medieval period, it also became an agricultural hub and local chieftains built a network of tanks along the Noyyal river to store water. In the nineteenth century, Coimbatore became a local administrative centre under British rule. However, by the beginning of the twentieth century, it had developed into a major textile cluster.

This industry continued to grow in independent India till, in the late 1990s, part of it shifted to the nearby town of Tiruppur (in the same district). Coimbatore town itself moved up the value chain into the engineering sector as well as into services such as education and transportation. At the same time, the city found itself at the heart of a network of towns, including Coonoor, Ooty, Palakkad, Tiruppur and Pollachi. Over time, there was urban growth along the roads linking these towns. Ribbons of unregulated construction now stretch along the highways. Thus, the impact of today's Coimbatore is not just about the town alone but the broader urban web that feeds it.

## IMPACT OF RAPID URBANISATION

The growth of Coimbatore and the surrounding network of towns has undoubtedly brought some economic prosperity. It is home to several wealthy industrial groups and has generated thousands of jobs for local and migrant workers. The population of Coimbatore town jumped from a mere

0.36 million in 1971 to over 1.5 million, but this understates the expansion as it does not include the wider network. However, the long-term environmental cost of this growth is now becoming evident. Here is just a sample of three inter-related issues:

- The Noyyal river and its network of tanks once provided the area with both drinking and irrigation water. A colonial-era survey map from 1906 suggests that the Noyyal, unusually for southern India, was a perennial river. Today, the river is almost completely dry by the time it reaches Coimbatore town. This is the result of the degradation of the mountain catchments, overuse for irrigation in the upper reaches, pumping of groundwater by bottling plants and so on.

- The Nilgiris and its foothills are some of the richest biodiversity hotspots in the world. Coimbatore's urban system is surrounded by wildlife sanctuaries such as Annamalai, Madhumalai, Bandipur and so on. There are forest areas within a few kilometres of Coimbatore town. These forests contain endangered species such as tigers, Asian elephants and the hornbill. Urban expansion is threatening their habitat, even ignoring encroachments and other illegal activities. Elephant migration corridors provide a good illustration of the problem. There are now busy highways that cut through these corridors. Brick kilns, residential homes, educational institutes and even theme parks are being built right up to the edge of the forest. As a result, the elephants are finding themselves stranded in scattered enclaves with inadequate water, food and mating opportunities. It is common to see a confused group of elephants in the middle of a highway without an escape route. Not surprisingly, man-animal conflict has spiralled out and people are being killed often by enraged pachyderms. Locals are responding by raising illegal and deadly electric fences.

- Urban growth and industrialisation generates both solid waste and sewage. The popular lake in Ooty is now full of sewage despite several clean-up initiatives. Similarly, plastic bags and packaging material are now scattered across the urban and rural landscape, and can now be found blowing deep inside the forests. In the few places that solid waste is collected, the disposal system mainly consists of open burning—which merely transfers the toxins into the air. Coimbatore is not unique in this, but the dispersed nature of urban growth makes it difficult to solve this with a centralised disposal system.

## WHAT CAN WE DO?

Urbanisation is not necessarily bad for the environment. What matters is urban form and the management of the commons. Coimbatore's urban web is based on sprawling along major roads. As more roads are built, the sprawl grows. This is not just environmentally harmful but is also economically inefficient. The solution lies in creating a network of dense urban hubs. One way to encourage this is by investing in rail rather than road links. A rail-based transport system would force denser clustering around the train stops unlike a road-based system. A colonial-era railway network already exists and should be modernised. The old hill train to Ooty, for instance, should not just be seen as a relic for tourists but as a practical and modern means of transport.

More broadly, we need to create mechanisms to manage the remaining commons. At the very least, we need to stop all illegal encroachments on forest land. However, we may also need to create buffer zones around water catchments and ecologically sensitive areas where land use is carefully managed. This is not a simple issue because it directly impinges upon private property rights. How does one convince a legitimate land-owner that she cannot build a wall around her property—especially when there is a risk that wild elephants could come rampaging through? Perhaps one should look at a compensation mechanism funded by rationally pricing residential and industrial water use in urban areas. Such a system has been successfully used by New York to preserve watersheds in the Catskill mountains. Another mechanism could be the creation of tradable development rights.

To conclude, the growth of small cities like Coimbatore is economically beneficial but still needs to be actively managed. This is especially true when it creates an urban sprawl near environmentally sensitive areas. Both the physical and regulatory infrastructure needs to be primed to guide urbanisation along a sustainable path.

(This piece was originally published in *Business Standard*, August 2010)

# SLUMS DEFY A 'CONCRETE' ANSWER

There is every sign that India is launching into a period of rapid urbanisation. In the next thirty years, an additional 350 million people will have to be accommodated in our existing towns as well as in brand new urban spaces. Given our inability to cater to even the existing urban population, there are serious concerns about our ability to deal with the influx. Are we entering a world of endless slums? The government has a plan to make India slum-free by 2015. Is this really good for the urban poor?

## RETHINKING SLUMS AS 'ROUTERS'

Economists and policymakers like to use terms like 'development'. However, at its heart, development really means the shifting of people from subsistence farming to other forms of livelihood. Urbanisation is the spatial mirror of this process. This is why virtually every developed country is urbanised. We can clearly see that a combination of changing job opportunities, aspirations and lifestyles is driving India's rural youth to flock to urban centres. The problem is to match hundreds of millions of migrants to jobs, housing and amenities while maintaining overall social cohesion. Slotting so many individuals into the urban fabric according to his/her skills and financial abilities is a colossal task.

China used draconian social control systems to manage the process over the last two decades. In most other countries, slums played this role. Even in China, 'urban villages' have been an integral part of the migration process.

Most people tend to be overwhelmed by the poor living conditions that prevail in Indian slums. The usual reaction is to treat this as a housing problem. Over the decades, we have seen many well-meaning slum re-development projects that have attempted to resettle slum-dwellers into concrete housing blocks (often on the outskirts of the city) and give them non-marketable property rights to their new homes. Yet, almost all of these efforts have failed to rid our cities of slums. More often than not, the former slum-dwellers either sell, rent out or abandon the new housing blocks and move back into a slum.

The problem is that these schemes take a static view of slums, whereas slums are really evolving ecosystems that include informal jobs inside the slum, access to employment outside the slum, social networks, ease of entry, security and so on. Thus, slums play an important role as 'routers' in the urbanisation process. They absorb poor migrants from the rural hinterland and naturalise them into the urban landscape. In doing so, they provide the urban economy with an army of blue-collar workers—maids, drivers, factory-workers etc.—who are essential for the functioning of any vibrant city. Urban master plans simply ignore this dynamic process and consequently are unable to deal with it.

## WHY ARE INDIAN SLUMS 'SAFE?'

Slums are not unique to India. Virtually every country has faced this problem in some form during its period of rapid development. The slums of New York and London were legendary in the nineteenth and early twentieth century. However, we need to distinguish between urban decay and slums. Urban decay describes the condition of blight, hopelessness and abandonment that one sees in New Jersey, northern England or even in parts of Africa and Latin America. As writers like Jeb Brugmann have pointed out, Indian slums are not places of hopelessness but of enterprise and energy. Whether it is Mumbai's Dharavi or Delhi's lal dora villages, most Indian slums have an astonishing variety of commercial activity, including shops, food vendors, garages and mini-factories.

Indeed, slums like Dharavi are remarkable in how safe and cohesive they are. Most of us will be able to walk through the average Indian slum even at night without fear of being harmed. This is more than one can ask of downtown Johannesburg or Camden, New Jersey. Contrary to popular wisdom, inequality of income and wealth appears to have little impact on crime and social envy. Mumbai has many social schisms: Hindus versus Muslims, Marathi-speakers versus Hindi-speakers and so on. However, the city suffers little conflict between the rich and the poor despite having the most extreme differences in wealth and income.

This cohesion comes from the fact that migrants do not view slum-life as a static state of deprivation, but as a foothold into the modern, urban economy. Life may be hard but, in a rapidly growing economy, there is enough socio-economic mobility to give most slum-dwellers hope and keep them hard-working, enterprising and law-abiding. This is being recognised even in China where the leading intellectual, Professor Qin Hui recently published a paper arguing that China needed more slums!

## WHAT SHOULD WE DO ABOUT SLUMS?

I am not arguing that slums do not need help. Clearly, we need to provide the urban poor with better sanitation, public health, education and so on. However, we need to rethink the framework of our interventions.

First, advocates of slum redevelopment should recognise that they are not just dealing with a housing problem but are tampering with a complex ecosystem. Thus, plans need to allow for informal commercial activities, public transport, and so on. To the extent possible, the redevelopment projects should be phased in a way that the ecosystems are not killed in the name of progress.

Second, we need to understand that slums are about ease of entry, upward mobility and churn. This process should not be disturbed by indiscriminately handing out non-marketable property rights. Instead, public intervention should encourage a market for rental accommodation starting from basic dormitories. However, when it is deemed appropriate to give property titles to slum-dwellers, the rights should be marketable.

Finally, and very importantly, we should not expect slums in the largest cities to act as routers for all the hundreds of millions of migrants. This is why we need to think of the small mofussil towns as mini-routers for the regional job markets. As I argued many times over, we need to revive small towns as social and economic hubs.

(This piece was originally published in *Business Standard*, January 2013)

# SMART CITIES ARE NOT ABOUT TECHNOLOGY

Around the world, there is a lot of discussion these days about smart cities. The Indian government, too, has been talking about building a hundred smart cities. But what are 'smart cities'? If one probes a little, one quickly discovers that the common perception is essentially about embedding the latest digital technologies—from sensors and Big Data to solar panels—in the master plan in order to optimise urban clusters. Smart city enthusiasts advocate that countries like India, that need to build new cities, should use the opportunity to hardwire the latest technology in the design.

While new technologies should certainly be deployed, should we define smartness purely in terms of the latest technology? Smart cities are not like smartphones that one can replace them when the next model becomes available. Cities last for centuries and their success depend on the ability to constantly adapt to new economic, social and technological contexts. Is there not a danger that we undermine long-term flexibility by single-minded pursuit of static optimisation?

In order to understand the dynamics of cities, one must first recognise that they are Complex Adaptive Systems just like natural ecosystems, macro-economic systems, weather systems and so on. This means that outcomes evolve from the complex interaction of constantly mutating elements. When managing such systems, one must first accept that there is no optimal 'equilibrium' that one should aspire for. This is why socialist economic planning and traditional urban master planning are bound to fail. They are based on a fundamental misconception about the state of the world.

This does not mean that one cannot improve outcomes through active management. Far from it, successful economies, wildlife reserves and urban centres are actively managed. However, the managers focus on very different things. One example is of property rights—even slums can evolve and upgrade themselves when property rights are clear. In contrast, squatter slums only change through external intervention. Surely then, the design of the intricate network of property rights, including that of the ownership and access to public spaces and infrastructure, should be a key element of 'smartness'. Sadly, it is not even a part of the debate.

Similarly, a key element that defines great urban hubs is the way people move around and interact. Everyone agrees that a public transport system is very important in this context, but the backbone of any such infrastructure is walking. After all, the first and last mile must be walked. Walking may be the most basic technology, but it is critical to smartness. Yet, it is not an important part of the smart city discussion.

It should be recognised, furthermore, that smart cities are ultimately about clustering smart people and not steel-and-chrome towers. Building human capital clusters also requires active management and investment. One obvious strategy is to weave educational, cultural and intellectual institutions into the fabric of the city. Yet, Indian urban planners are doing exactly the opposite. Universities are not being built as part of the city but as large stand-alone islands outside the city. This is not just a waste of land and amenities, but also gets in the way of creating clusters. Similarly, the smart city advocates say little about the need to make space for museums, think tanks, theatres, temples, sports facilities or iconic buildings. No amount of digital technology can create a human capital cluster without investing in such cultural and intellectual institutions.

Even if all the above elements are taken into account, long-term success depends ultimately on flexibility. There are currently several attempts to build smart cities from scratch. Perhaps the most ambitious is Masdar City being built at great expense near Abu Dhabi. The city's designers have taken care, in theory at least, to include walkability and social interaction in the planning. However, the real focus of the experiment is to hardwire the latest digital technology into the urban landscape. My concern is that even if the project is finished and then populated, the city could become outdated within a decade of going live. A Complex Adaptive System evolves by constantly adjusting to random, unpredictable mutations. A fully integrated and internally consistent system will have great difficulty dealing with this organic phenomenon.

Let me clarify that I am not a Luddite who is against deploying new technology. I am merely arguing that technology is a useful tool for achieving other objectives and is not a goal in itself. For instance, property rights can greatly benefit from digital records and mapping. Walking systems can similarly be optimised using video mapping and Big Data to analyse how people move around a city. Singapore, perhaps the closest we have to an existing smart city, uses an elaborate system of electric road pricing to manage traffic congestion. However, note that it simultaneously invests in building and populating new theatres, museums, universities and stadiums. In recent years, I have been personally involved in an effort to map and create new cycling and pedestrian paths in the city. Great care is taken to ensure that these institutions and infrastructure are not islands of excellence, but feed into the overall urban fabric.

In short, the government's smart city project must not get hijacked by technological derring-do. Smart cities are really about bringing together smart human capital and institutions.

(This piece was originally published in *Business Standard*, April 2015)

# THOSE STREETS ARE MADE FOR WALKING

More than half the world's population lives in cities and, within a generation, this will be true even for India. How we design and run our cities is important for virtually every aspect of human activity in the twenty-first century. Not surprisingly, therefore, we expect our cities to do many things at the same time. We expect them to be energy-efficient and environment-friendly. We want them to be socially inclusive. We also need them to be vibrant engines of economic growth. Are these contradictory goals or is there a way to maximise them simultaneously?

The good news is that there is a design paradigm that is simple, low-cost and combines all these goals. The bad news is that Indian urban planning almost entirely ignores it. The design paradigm is 'walkability' and, as we shall see, it is far more important than flyovers, metro-trains and other expensive solutions to urban problems.

Walkability is about urban design that allows people to use walking (perhaps combined with cycling) as an important, if not dominant, means of getting around. Thus, people should be able to walk to work, as well as walk to urban amenities like schools, parks, restaurants and shops. Obviously, walking cannot be the only means of urban mobility, especially in a large city. However, urban design can be oriented to walking as a way of life, including linkages to other forms of transport, such as buses, trains and so on.

## WHY WALKABILITY?

Some of the most successful cities in the world invest a large amount of effort in ensuring walkability—New York, Boston, Singapore, Amsterdam, Paris and so on. Seoul has torn down a motorway in the middle of the city and turned it into a pedestrian-friendly path along a revived stream. New York has converted old, elevated rail tracks in Lower Manhattan into a walking path. Singapore has created a network of underground passages in its business and shopping districts connected to its Mass Rapid Transit system. Even hilly Hong Kong uses a combination of elevated walkways and escalators to connect its business district. All of these interventions have proved very popular. Why do these rich and advanced cities invest heavily in such a basic form of mobility?

First, walking and cycling are the most environment-friendly means of getting around. Moreover, they are essential for the functioning of all other forms of public transport because the first and last mile of all public transport systems must usually be walked. This is commonly ignored by Indian urban planners. New metro stations and bus stops are created but without any way for the commuter to then walk to her final destination.

Second, walking is the most socially inclusive means of transport. Both rich and poor can walk, and they must use the same public space. This creates social interaction and an egalitarian culture. When applied to a smaller scale—say, to a small town or a neighbourhood—walking creates a sense of community and greater engagement with civic issues. It is not as easy to walk past an overflowing drain or a reeking garbage dump as it is to drive past them.

Third, walking has large economic benefits that are usually ignored. It is now widely recognised that much of the economic dynamism of urban agglomerations come from their ability to generate random and frequent interactions between people. This is what creates business networks, encourages the exchange of ideas and triggers creativity (what is often called urban buzz). Research has shown that this is still best done face-to-face and cannot be efficiently done over the phone or the Internet. Walkability is critical to this process. The street cafes of Paris, the walk along Charles River in Boston and the University Parks in Oxford have generated far more ideas than the best of laboratories. This is why the finance industry, the most networked of sectors, still thinks it worthwhile to be concentrated in a tiny area around Wall Street and the City of London.

I have just discussed a few of the benefits of walkability. There are many more, including improvements in general health. I am not persuaded by the argument that India's heat makes walking infeasible. Singapore is hot and humid throughout the year and it rains there almost every day. Yet, the city is a wonderful place to walk because of thoughtful design.

## HOW TO DESIGN FOR IT?

Let me clarify that 'walkability' is not just about building more pedestrian footpaths. It requires a combination of over/underpasses, pavements, safe crossings, public spaces like parks and so on. It also needs supporting infrastructure like public toilets, signages, security systems and access for the physically challenged. However, walkability requires a number of fundamental changes in urban form in order to work. Let me list out a few:

- Density: Walking cannot work in a spread-out suburbia even if there are lots of pedestrian paths. Thus, walkability presupposes a dense urban form. This has the additional benefit that it reduces the use of land and, consequently, further lowers the environmental footprint.

- Mixed use: Walkability needs a mix-and-match urban form where there is an ecosystem of urban activity and amenities. We need to abandon industrial-era zoning still loved by Indian planners. In fact, next generation urban design should even design for the phenomenon such as street vendors (properly regulated) in order to make the walking experience more interesting.

- Public transport and taxis: Walking has one big disadvantage that it is limited by the human body. This is why it is very important that walking and cycling are consciously integrated into the public transport network. Note that a well-functioning taxi system is critical. People will take to walking only if they know that there is a reliable alternative whenever the situation demands it.

Sadly, very little attention is paid to walkability as a design paradigm in India and other developing countries. Instead, new cities are being built on outdated visions of American suburbia. Large sums are still being spent to 'widen roads'—a euphemism for narrowing the pedestrian sidewalk. Massive flyovers and highways are being built without any thought to how pedestrians can cross them. The time has come to stand up for the hapless Mr Walker.

(This piece was originally published in *Business Standard*, June 2010)

# THE ART OF PUBLIC HOUSING

The government's plan to make India 'slum free' is taking shape. Peruvian economist, Hernando de Soto is being roped in to provide inputs. An ambitious scheme called the Rajiv Awas Yojana is being designed. This is a very important area because it goes to the crux of how to accommodate 300-400 million people in urban India in the next three decades. The urbanisation process will redefine the country within a generation and we need to get it right. In an earlier piece (see, Slums Defy a 'Concrete' Answer, p. 160) I have argued that we need to think of slums as 'routers' in the migration process and that the property rights of the urban poor are not just about real estate ownership. In this essay, I will look at the critical role that public housing can play in guiding the urbanisation process.

Public housing is not a new idea and various versions of it have been tried across the world. However, it must be remembered that it has very rarely been a wholesale success. In many cases, it has created ghettos of poverty and despondency. In others, the rich have captured the projects and have benefited from the subsidies. One of the few exceptions is Singapore where public housing projects played a very important role in transforming the city-state within a generation from a poor, slum-riddled port to one of the world's most prosperous and advanced cities. What makes it even more impressive is that this was achieved by the mobilisation of internal resources and not the deployment of a windfall from oil or some other natural resource.

## THE SINGAPORE STORY

In the early 1960s, Singapore suffered from severe housing shortages. A large section of the population lived in unhygienic squatter camps that were prone to frequent fires and communal tensions. In a single fire at Bukit Ho Swee in 1961, several people were killed and 16,000 people were rendered homeless. The race riots of July 1964 left twenty-three people dead and hundreds injured. In other words, life in Singapore's slums was no better than in slums that we see in Indian cities today.

The British-run colonial government decided to set up the Housing and Development Board (HDB) in 1960. The agency had built over 54,000 housing units by the time Singapore became independent in 1965. In the initial phase, the flats were basic and were meant for renting. Over time, the quality and choice of housing were increased even as schemes were introduced to help people buy their homes. An important financing innovation in 1968 was to allow citizens to use money from the Central Provident Fund for down payments and servicing.

HDB housing grew very rapidly in the 1970s and 1980s. In tandem with this growth, the government invested heavily in common amenities such as health, education and public transport. Special efforts were made to accommodate small businesses as well as community hubs, such as sports facilities and places of worship.

Today, about eighty per cent of Singaporeans live in HDB housing and ninety-five per cent own homes. It is extraordinary that the citizens of one of the world's most prosperous cities choose to live in public housing.

## WHAT CAN WE LEARN?

I have found that Indian urban experts arrogantly dismiss Singapore as a small-scale experiment. I disagree. Singapore is a small country but it is a reasonably large city of over five million—larger than all but six Indian cities. It has been able to raise the standards of living of its population dramatically in a very dense urban environment purely through internally generated resources. This is why, for the last two decades, a string of Chinese mayors have swallowed their pride and made a pilgrimage to the city-state. I know that Singapore's public housing policies cannot be blindly applied to India, but there are some important principles that are universal and worthy of consideration:

- Clear property rights are very important for creating a sense of ownership. However, note that there is a big difference in the Singaporean approach and that of Hernando de Soto. The latter is in favour of regularising squatter rights whereas the Singaporeans preferred to wipe the slate clean using public acquisition of land. From the Singaporean viewpoint, regularising squatter rights would reward squatting and ultimately undermine the very basis of property rights.

- Public housing may be partly subsidised but it should not be too cheap—and never free. Instead, there is a housing ladder which starts with cheap rentals and ends in high-end condominium apartments like those in the Pinnacle complex. In other words, the urban poor are not seen as a static group in need of handouts. The underlying assumption is that people have aspirations and they will work hard and climb the ladder quite quickly if given the chance. This is very different from de Soto's world of small holdings and micro-finance, where the poor improve their situation in tiny incremental steps. Perhaps the difference in world view reflects the difference between the rapid growth experience of Asia and the slow growth of Latin America.

- Management of the commons is critical. Thus, the Singaporean approach invests very heavily in common amenities, public transport, maintenance and so on. Residents of HDB estates are made to pay a small management fee every month. Similarly, every effort is made to cluster economic and social nodes within each HDB estate. Even informal sector activities like hawker-centres are designed into the public housing system. Again, this is very different from de Soto's approach that focuses on private ownership of property and largely ignores the commons.

- Real estate laws are transparent and evenly applied by a quick legal system. This is a necessary corollary of properly defined property rights. This is one area where the Singaporeans and Hernando de Soto would strongly agree with each other.

The purpose of this essay is to point out that there is an 'Asian model' for thinking about public housing and slum upgrade. This does not mean that rock star economists like de Soto should be ignored. He clearly has ideas that should be considered seriously. I merely hope that the Indian government will weigh various options before embarking on an important and expensive project.

(This piece was originally published in *Business Standard*, January 2013)

# URBAN PLANNING AND CHAOS

The high-powered committee headed by Dr Isher Judge Ahluwalia recently presented its report on urban infrastructure. The report focuses on the infrastructure needs of a rapidly urbanising country and highlights important issues ranging from governance to waste management. I have high personal regard for individual members of the committee and find few faults with specific recommendations. My disagreement with this and other such reports is on the grounds that they read like laundry lists rather than strategic documents. This is the result of a flawed philosophical approach to deal with organic systems like cities.

## THE THEORY OF CHAOS

The basic approach of the high-powered committee was to identify specific problems and systematically resolve each of them. This may appear very sensible, but cities are complex systems that do not lend themselves to such a mechanical approach. The reader may feel that my criticism of the urban infrastructure report is a case of philosophical hair-splitting, but I would request them to indulge me with a small detour into the theory of chaotic systems.

This is a world of non-linear and evolving dynamics, multiple and changing equilibrium, increasing returns to scale and complex feedback loops. Weird as these may sound, they describe many things we see in real life such as weather systems, financial markets, evolving economies and, of course, cities. Modern science is all about dealing with such phenomena. Even the lay reader would have heard of the Heisenberg Uncertainty Principle and of the famous image of how the fluttering of butterfly wings can ultimately cause a hurricane. This is why the suicide of a street vendor in Tunisia could bring down governments across the Arab world.

However, chaotic systems are not random. They may not be deterministic, but there are many interesting patterns, probabilities and characteristics that can be exploited when dealing with them. Weather forecasting is a good example of an area where science has developed a dramatically better understanding in recent decades. It may never be possible to pinpoint weather, but we can now say quite a lot about it.

Note how the dynamics of the chaotic universe are fundamentally different from the Newtonian world of levers and pulleys. It is over a hundred years since the natural sciences have moved away from the mechanical worldview. Yet social scientists have persisted with the old thinking process. Socialist economic planning and rigid master planning of cities are accepted as failures, but the basic process remains embedded in our policy making. Thus, recommendations of Dr Ahluwalia's report eventually boil down to increasing spending allocations to a new and enlarged version of the Jawaharlal Nehru Urban Renewal Mission.

## 'CHAOTIC WORLD' POLICIES

There are many interesting implications of thinking of the world in chaotic terms. First, the dynamics of a chaotic system depend on history, time and point of origin. This implies that the timing, angle and point of intervention matter more than the force applied. Less can often mean more. The conventional response to a traffic problem today is that we need more 'infrastructure'—which implies more flyovers and other hardware. Yet, we know from experience that most flyovers merely redistribute the traffic jam. In contrast, better traffic policing would be far cheaper and provide immediate results.

Second, in the chaotic universe, the overall ecosystem is more than the sum of its parts. Thus, chaotic systems are defined by the dynamics of clustering and increasing returns to scale. Singapore's urban strategy is a successful illustration of this principle. Over the last decade, Singapore has emerged as Asia's leading 'Global City'. This was achieved by investing in the strangest of things—urban buzz. The Singaporeans deliberately clustered an odd mix of things in the middle of the city—malls, a new university, a casino, theatres, offices, museums, residential apartments, hotels and even a Formula One circuit. None of these would have worked in isolation, but the combination created an exciting ecosystem that generates thousands of jobs and billions of dollars of economic activity. Although Dr Ahluwalia's report has sensibly moved away from rigid urban master planning, it's still about a list of ingredients and not about the cooking.

In defence of Dr Ahluwalia's high-powered committee, its report merely reflects a worldview that is embedded in Indian policy-making and is common even abroad. A good global example is the response of international financial regulators to the recent financial crisis. As already mentioned, financial markets are also chaotic systems. Thus, more regulation does not mean better regulation. After all, the financial system was very heavily regulated even before the crisis, and yet the crisis was not prevented. How will more regulations help? Ever more complex regulations will make the system more opaque and make it even more prone to future crises. It is far better to have simple and clear regulations backed up by active management. There is no regulatory framework that can substitute for constant human monitoring and judgement.

This is also true for cities. Indian cities need hard infrastructure, but ultimately they are not about buildings, roads and sewage drains, but about people and their varied social and economic interactions. In its pursuit of civil engineering and hardware, Indian urban thinking simply ignores the human software that brings cities alive. Ultimately, the future of Indian cities will be decided by the process of human capital clustering and interaction, a sense of place and belonging and, most importantly, the spirit of innovation and enterprise. This is why the most important infrastructure of a city relates to property rights, access to commons, municipal transparency, clustering of social amenities, upward mobility and so on.

(This piece was originally published in *Business Standard*, April 2011)

# HOW RATIONAL IS DELHI'S ROAD RATIONING

A big debate on urban transport policy has been triggered by the decision of the Delhi government to restrict automobile usage according to the licence plate number. The plan is to significantly reduce vehicular traffic by allowing odd and even numbers to ply the roads on alternate days. Given the city's atrocious air quality, something drastic needs to be done. The problem is that this particular policy has been tried in other countries for years with poor results except for short periods. The danger is that a focus on implementing this policy will divert attention from more serious solutions.

The idea of using the licence plate number to ration road space is not new. It was used by the Chinese authorities during the Beijing Olympics to improve air quality and is said to have had some impact. A more permanent restriction called *Hoy No Circula* (No Circulating Day) was introduced in Mexico City in 1989 that banned drivers from using their car once a week based on the licence plate number. Different versions were subsequently adopted by other Latin American cities like Bogota and Sao Paulo. Again, there were clear short-term benefits. Mexico City, for instance, saw a twenty per cent reduction in vehicular traffic in the first few months.

Unfortunately, the longer-term outcomes were not so encouraging. A study of air quality impact published in 2007 by Lucas Davis of the University of Michigan concluded:

> Across pollutants and specifications there is no evidence that the program has improved air quality. The policy has caused a relative increase in air pollution during weekends and weekday hours when the restrictions are not in place, but there is no evidence of an absolute improvement in air quality during any period of the week for any pollutant.

It turns out that people begin to game the system once it's permanent. Mexico City residents began to buy extra cars with convenient number plates. In fact, they slowed down the purchase of new cars and began to buy old, inefficient cars from the rest of the country. This actually made things worse. Moreover, the shift in the mode of transportation was from cars to taxis rather than to metro trains. Thus, the taxis made more money, but the air quality did not improve. After two months of implementation, petrol sales went up. Based on these findings, a technical study commissioned by New York City argued against introducing such a system in 2007.

The Delhi government has announced that it will do a trial run from the beginning of January 2016. My guess is that the trial will show some positive results that can be misleading as it will provide no indication of how Delhiites will adjust their behaviour to a permanent imposition. It is almost certain that the rich will buy multiple cars to get around the restrictions and the extra idle cars will lead to a parking nightmare in residential neighbourhoods. An additional problem will soon arise over what to do with cars from other states. If the same restriction is not placed on them, Delhiites will just register cars in other states. However, the imposition of the restriction on non-Delhi cars will cause problems for visitors who genuinely happen to be visiting the city for a short duration. If not sensibly handled, it will spiral into an inter-state spat.

A key condition for the success of road rationing is that alternatives are easily available. The building of Delhi Metro has certainly improved public transport in the city and buses are now much better than the old DTC (Delhi Transport Corporation) clunkers. However, the frequency and network are still far from adequate and, on many routes, the services are running at full capacity. There is an even bigger problem that is almost never discussed—the appalling state of pedestrian infrastructure. All public transport systems are based on the last and first mile being walked. This is not only about sidewalks but also crossings, street-lighting, cleanliness, the removal of feral animals and so on. Safety for women is a particular concern. Having studied public transport systems around the world, I can say that walkability is by far the most serious bottleneck to the use of public transport in Delhi (and most other Indian cities).

Meanwhile, the Delhi government may consider other alternatives. Singapore, for instance, uses a system of auctioned permits and electronic road pricing. Thus, the restriction is based on price rather than on rationing. Cars are charged as they drive around the city and the pricing varies on the location and time of day. Such a system will require some upfront investment in technology but the outcome will be vastly better and give car users a lot more flexibility. Perhaps Delhi could even leapfrog into a more advanced GPS-based system.

Delhi clearly needs a solution but it makes no sense to rush into a system with a dubious international record. The danger is that it will use up a lot of resources and energy that could be better aimed at other solutions—such as fixing pedestrian networks.

(This piece was originally published in *Mint*, December 2015)

# WHY INDIAN CITIES NEED FLEXIBLE PLANS

India is urbanising rapidly and it appears that the country will have an urban majority within a generation. With our cities and towns already struggling, the management of rapid urban expansion will remain one of our most important challenges over the next decade. However, whenever this issue is raised, the inevitable consensus is that the solution lies in 'better planning'. But what does 'better planning' really mean?

If one pushes people to articulate what they mean by better planning, my experience is that sooner or later they will bring up the example of Singapore; if only Indian cities were as well planned as the city-state. So the obvious next question is: which Indian city comes closest to the Singaporean ideal? Two-thirds of the responses will include Chandigarh. It may not be as successful as Singapore, but everyone is sure that it is well planned. The irony is that Singapore's approach is the exact opposite of Chandigarh's planning, and the mix-up is at the root of urban failure in India.

Chandigarh is now a sixty-year-old mature city but its urban structure is still based on a master plan drawn up by Le Corbusier in the 1950s. Indeed, officials take great pride in the extent to which today's urban landscape adheres to the original master plan. This reflects the thinking that good urban development is about creating a brilliant plan and then implementing it as meticulously as possible.

It sounds like a reasonable approach and is reflected in all organised Indian urban expansion since Independence: Navi Mumbai, Kolkata's Bidhan Nagar (Salt Lake), Durgapur, Gandhinagar, Dispur and so on. None of them, however, has yet created a successful urban hub after two generations of trying, and India still depends on colonial-era cities. Meanwhile, the boom-towns of Bengaluru and Gurugram continue to grow by ignoring all the rudiments of planning. So, is there an alternative way of thinking about cities?

I have had the opportunity to work closely with Singapore's urban managers for many years and the most striking difference with the Indian approach is that the Singaporeans take their plans less seriously. Instead, they see them as working frameworks of reference that evolve along with the city. This is analogous to how successful entrepreneurs use business plans. This may come as a big surprise to people who see the city-state as the epitome of meticulous planning.

The Singaporean approach is based on the idea that the city is a living ecosystem. One can make strategic interventions and try to guide it in a particular way but the city will keep evolving in different, often unexpected, ways. The focus is on managing this process and constantly adapting rather than sticking to some preconceived ideal endpoint. This is how Singapore has gone from British naval outpost to container shipment port, then from electronics manufacturing cluster to financial centre, and most recently to education and entertainment hub. During the same period, Chandigarh's urban managers focused on being true to Corbusier's original plan.

So, what lessons can be learnt from this alternative approach? First, the organic approach to planning is about thinking out scenarios and building in optionality rather than meticulously laying out an ideal end-state. There is nothing sacred about the 'master plan'.

Second, one must accept that some urban interventions will succeed while others will fail; yet others will have unintended consequences. Many of Singapore's urban interventions fail, but the authorities systematically shut down failed or outdated projects. This requires constant and dispassionate monitoring. The implication is that a constant updating of the real city's map is more important than the idealised map of the master plan.

Third, the focus should be on managing constant transitions rather than on reaching an end-point. This may seem obvious, but this is different from the usual Indian approach of blaming bad planning rather than bad management. Even a mediocre plan can lead to an acceptable outcome if the city is managed well, but even the best plan cannot work without decent management.

I have used Singapore to illustrate my point but my

interaction with the urban authorities of other rapidly changing cities, from Dubai to Shanghai, suggests that they all value flexibility much more than Indians. They also place greater emphasis on mapping ground reality in contrast to Indian civic authorities, who treat the official plan as if it is reality.

Of course, the flexible approach has its own downsides—for instance, iconic buildings are torn down routinely in Singapore when they no longer serve a practical purpose. However, the purpose of contrasting the two approaches is to show how India's cities, contrary to popular belief, suffer from too much belief in planning and not enough emphasis on management. India needs to focus on managing Gurugram and Bengaluru better rather than dreaming of another Chandigarh.

(This piece was originally published in *Mint*, February 2017)

# VILLAGES THAT LIVE IN OUR CITIES

As our cities have expanded over the years, they have absorbed the surrounding agricultural lands. In some cases, the old villages too have been swept away. However, in most cases, the old villages survive despite being engulfed by the expanding urban sprawl. Scattered across modern Indian cities, there remain enclaves where the contours of the old villages can be clearly discerned decades after the surrounding farmlands were converted into offices, roads, houses and shops. In some ways, this is a distinctive aspect of Indian civilisation—the ability to allow the past to live in the present. Yet, these urban villages have dramatically changed with the times. Despite being ignored by civic authorities, they play an important role in the evolving social and economic life of Indian cities.

## CHANGING WITH THE TIMES

There are urban villages in most Indian cities, often tucked away behind a modern building complex. They make their presence felt in many different ways—as the source of vagrant cattle, as homes to armies of informal workers, as the place to visit if one wants to buy bathroom tiles or electrical fittings. Many of these villages have been newly absorbed into the urban fabric, but some are old and have been embedded in the city for generations. In Mumbai, the old villages of Bandra and Walkeshwar retain strong vestiges of their origins despite being located at the heart of a throbbing megalopolis.

For the purposes of this essay, I will limit myself to Delhi's experience, although the story can be easily generalised. According to architect Ranjit Sabikhi, there are 106 villages within the city-state. They are many more in the wider metropolitan area if one includes NOIDA and Gurugram. My studies suggest that, in general, these villages go through the following cycle:

- The farmers sell their land to the government or to a developer. Some of them fritter away their newly acquired wealth, but most redeploy it in businesses that leverage the emerging urban landscape— transportation, labour contracting, supply of construction material and so on. Some of the more prosperous villagers buy themselves new homes and move out. However, they all usually retain their houses in the old village settlement. This settlement, dubbed as a lal dora area, is exempt from usual municipal and building codes. The ex-farmers use the exemption to build a mishmash of buildings with little regard for safety or ventilation. These become home to construction workers and other service providers who move into the area. Thus, the village turns into a slum with the old villagers as slum-lords.

• After about a decade, construction work in that particular area begins to wind down. The construction workers drift away to other sites. New migrants move in—security guards, maids, drivers and other people who work in the newly built urban space. The commercial establishments too go through a parallel transformation. The shops selling construction material and hardware are steadily replaced by shops selling mobile phones, street food, car parts and so on. For the first time, we see private and, occasionally public, investment in amenities such as common toilets. As the migrants become more permanent, they bring in their families from their ancestral villages. This leads to an interesting supply-side response—the 'English Medium' school! In my experience, language is seen by the poor as the single most important tool for social climbing. Nathupur in Gurugram is an example of a village that is currently moving from the first stage to the second stage. Next door, the village of Sikandarpur is slowly shifting to the next stage.

• After another ten to fifteen years, the village goes

through yet another transformation. By this time, the surrounding area is well-settled and open agricultural fields are a distant memory. We now see students, salesmen and small businessmen move into the village. Some of them may be the newly educated children of migrants, but they are now a higher social class. The old villagers still continue to be the dominant owners of the land, but they now begin to invest in improving their individual properties in order to elicit higher rents (after all, they now have a location advantage in the middle of the growing city). In many instances, the owners have become politically important to lobby for public investment in basic drainage and sanitation. In my experience, public transport connections have a strong positive effect on the economic dynamism of the slum. The shops upgrade themselves and the old street food sellers become cheap restaurants. An 'Aggarwal Sweets' is almost obligatory in the larger settlements.

- The final stage in the process of transformation is that the old village gentrifies. This can happen in a number of ways. Since the early Nineties, Hauz Khas village has become a warren of boutique shops, art galleries and trendy restaurants. Mahipalpur, near the international airport, has seen an explosion of cheap hotels in the last decade. Similarly, Shahpur Jat has become home to numerous small offices and designer workshops. In many cases, the old villagers have encashed their real estate and the ownership pattern has become much more mixed. The areas now grapple with the problems of prosperity such as inadequate parking.

## WHAT CAN WE LEARN?

The evolution of urban villages reminds us that Indian slums are not places of hopelessness, but are often industrious and changing ecosystems. The process of evolution has a big positive impact on the economic and social development of both the old villagers as well as new migrants. However, there are two important learnings. First, public investment in the commons speeds up the development process. Amenities such as common toilets, public transport and drainage can have an important impact on the quality of life of residents as well as attract new economic opportunities. Second, the process of adaptation depends on decades of steady investment by the owners. This is only possible because private property rights are clear. This is why the same process of evolution does not easily take root in squatter slums. Policy-makers must take these into account as they plan interventions aimed at making India 'slum-free'.

(This piece was originally published in *Business Standard,* January 2013)

# PROPERTY RIGHTS FOR FUTURE MIGRANTS

In his recent Budget speech, the finance minister reiterated the government's plans to make India 'slum-free' within five years. This mantra is now being chanted in many urban-related conferences. However, this raises a number of questions. What does a 'slum-free' India really mean? Is the removal of slums really desirable? Most importantly, what needs to be done to improve the lives of the millions of urban poor? In this piece, I have argued that public policy should focus less on getting rid of slums and more on rethinking property rights, especially those of the poor.

## THE FLOW OF URBAN POOR

The conventional view for making our cities slum-free is that we should build low-cost housing and shift the existing slum-dwellers into them. There is a serious flaw in this solution because the urban poor are not a static group but a flow.

In the last two years, I have travelled across many parts of rural India. The message is very clear. The children of farmers no longer want to stay on in their farms. No government scheme is going to hold back the change in aspirations. The country's cities need to prepare for the influx. In an earlier essay (see, Slums Defy a 'Concrete' Answer, p. 160) I had argued that slums play an important role in the phase of rapid urbanisation by absorbing and naturalising the new migrants into the urban landscape. As hundreds of millions of people are absorbed into urban India, slums and small mofussil towns will be needed as routers in this process. If we simply get rid of today's slums, we will merely get new ones.

The point is that we should concentrate on alleviating urban poverty rather than getting rid of slums. The former is the problem and the latter is merely the symptom. Peruvian economist Hernando de Soto has been arguing for years that the solution lies in strengthening the property rights of the poor. This is usually interpreted as formalisation of squatter rights. This may make sense in Latin America, which has a relatively stable population of urban poor and whose economy is growing slowly. However, this is too narrow an interpretation for a high-growth economy like India where booming urban centres are sucking in millions of new migrants.

The first problem with recognising squatter rights is that we create problems of governance by potentially encouraging land-grab. We not only have to think about today's urban poor, but also about the incentive structure presented to the next generation of migrants. Second, the formalisation is usually done on the basis of a cut-off date. This often recognises the rights of better off old-timers against those of poorer newcomers. Finally, and most importantly, in next generation cities like Gurugram the poor live in the 'urban villages' where property rights are very clearly defined and any tampering would cause serious social upheaval. So, what should we do?

## IDENTITY AS A PROPERTY RIGHT

The single-most important, and sometimes only, asset of a poor migrant is her identity. Without any form of identification, it is very difficult for a newcomer to fit into the urban landscape—no gas connection, no mobile phone, no voter rights, no credit and so on. It is nearly impossible for such an individual to apply for jobs in the formal economy or sometimes even as domestic help. Thus, a reliable and robust system of identification is invaluable. This is why Nandan Nilekeni's Unique Identity Number scheme may turn out to be a major intervention.

## ACCESS TO THE 'COMMONS'

The urban poor rely heavily on the commons to lead their lives. Therefore, much of their property rights relate to access to public amenities rather than to private space.

These include access to public transport, public toilets, public health, parks/open spaces, pedestrian networks and so on. These user rights are far more important to the poor than merely providing a housing solution for the individual. Urban design and public investment needs to be reoriented to focus on the commons.

## LEGAL INFRASTRUCTURE

All rights, including property rights, exist only within a legal framework. Urban laws and their application need to be oriented towards protecting the legitimate needs of the urban poor, especially in areas related to livelihood. For instance, street hawkers need to be recognised and incorporated into the legal and architectural framework of the city. Rather than see hawkers merely as a nuisance, we should see them as part of the ecosystem of a vibrant city. What they need is transparent regulation not banishment. The current approach taken by most municipal authorities is merely leading to the proliferation of illegal hawkers and to corruption.

If these frameworks are put in place, the urban poor will themselves find ways to move up the value chain. Indeed, the slums themselves will evolve and upgrade (as is happening anyway in many of the older urban villages of Delhi).

To conclude, we need to strengthen property rights that can be leveraged by the pipeline of future migrants. In Latin America, it may make sense to interpret property rights as mostly relating to land titles and squatter rights.

The population of urban poor in Latin America is relatively static—the countries are already fairy urbanised and their economies are growing slowly. In India, the throbbing economy is sucking millions of new migrants. We need to think of property rights in ways that allow these new migrants to enter and climb the system.

(This piece was originally published in *Business Standard*, March 2010)

# THE DETROIT SYNDROME

When the city of Detroit filed for bankruptcy last week, it became the largest such filing in United States' history. Detroit's population has dropped from 1.8 million in 1950, when it was America's fifth largest city, to less than 7,00,000 today. Its industrial base lies shattered.

And yet we live in a world where cities have never had it so good. More than half of the world's population is urban, for the first time in history, and urban hubs generate an estimated eighty per cent of global GDP. These proportions will rise even higher as emerging-market countries urbanise rapidly. So, what can the world learn from Detroit's plight?

As recently as the 1990s, many experts were suggesting that technology would make cities irrelevant. It was believed that the Internet and mobile communications, then infant technologies, would make it unnecessary for people to live in crowded and expensive urban hubs. Instead, cities like New York and London have experienced sharp increases in population since 1990, after decades of decline.

One factor that has helped cities is the nature of twenty-first century life. Previously, life in developed countries was based on daily routines: people went to work in offices and factories, returned home to eat dinner with their families, watched their favourite television programmes, went to sleep, and repeated the cycle when they awoke.

Such regular cycles no longer apply to most peoples' lives. In the course of a work day, people mix and match many activities—they may work at a desk, but they may also meet a friend for lunch, go to the gym, do chores, travel on business, shop online, and so on.

Similarly, time at home is no longer clearly demarcated, with people working online or participating in conference calls even as they manage their family life. We have discovered that this multi-tasking life is best done in cities, which concentrate on a multiplicity of hard amenities—airports, shops, schools, parks, and sports facilities—as well as soft amenities like clubs, bars, and restaurants.

Another factor is that cities have increased in importance as hubs for innovation and creativity. Until the nineteenth century, innovation was carried out mostly by generalists and tinkerers, which meant that the accumulation of new knowledge was slow, but that its diffusion across different fields was rapid. In the twentieth century, knowledge creation became the job of specialists, which accelerated knowledge creation but retarded inter-disciplinary application.

But recent studies have shown that this source of innovation is rapidly decelerating (the productivity of an American research worker may now be less than fifteen per cent of a similar researcher in 1950). Instead, innovation is increasingly based on mixing and matching knowledge from different specialisations. Certain cities are ideally suited for this, because they concentrate on different kinds of human capital and encourage random interactions between people with different knowledge and skills.

The problem with this post-industrial urban model is that it strongly favours generalist cities that can cluster different kinds of soft and hard amenities and human capital. Indeed, the growth dynamic can be so strong for some successful cities that they can hollow out smaller rivals (for example, London vis-à-vis the cities of northern England).

Some specialist cities could also do well in this world. But, as Detroit, with its long dependence on the automotive industry, demonstrates, cities that are dependent on a single industry or on a temporary location advantage may fare extremely poorly.

All of this has important implications for emerging economies. As it transformed itself into the 'factory of the world', the share of China's urban population jumped from 26.4 per cent in 1990 to around fifty-three per cent today. The big, cosmopolitan cities of Beijing and Shanghai have grown dramatically, but the bulk of the urban migration has been to cookie-cutter small and medium-sized industrial towns that have mushroomed over the last decade. By clustering industrial infrastructure and using the Hukou system of city-specific residency permits, the authorities have been able to control the process rather well.

This process of urban growth, however, is about to unravel. As China shifts its economic model away from heavy infrastructure investment and bulk manufacturing, many of these small industrial cities will lose their core industry. This will happen at a time when the country's skewed demographics causes the workforce to shrink and the flow of migration from rural areas to cities to slow down (the rural population now disproportionately comprises the elderly).

Meanwhile, the post-industrial attractions of cities like Shanghai and Beijing will attract the more talented and better-educated children of today's industrial workers. Unlike rural migrants heading for industrial jobs, it will be much more difficult to guide educated and creative professionals using the Hukou system. The boom in the successful cities, therefore, will hollow out human capital from less attractive industrial hubs, which will then fall into a vicious cycle of decay and falling productivity.

Stories like Detroit's have played out several times in developed countries during the last half century. And, as the fate of Mexico's northern towns suggests, emerging economies are not immune from this process.

That is why China needs to prepare for this moment. Rather than building ever more cookie-cutter industrial towns, China needs to refit and upgrade its existing cities. As its population begins to shrink, it may even be worthwhile to shut down unviable cities and consolidate. Detroit's fate should serve as a warning, not only for China, but for the next generation of urbanising countries (for example, India) as well.

(This piece was originally published in *Project Syndicate*, July 2013)

# SINGAPORE'S NEXT FRONTIER

In the last week of September, Singapore's government announced that the city-state's population now stood at 5.4 million and emphasised that the rate of immigration had slowed to the lowest level in a decade. While this is a routine announcement at one level, it comes at a time when demographics are at the centre of a national debate.

Singapore has exhibited extraordinary flexibility as it evolved, in a little more than a generation, from a British colonial outpost into one of the most successful cities in the world. At each stage, a visionary political leadership was able to add a new layer to the economy as it moved up the value chain—from a trading port to a manufacturing cluster, then a financial centre and, more recently, a hub for education, research and entertainment. However, the city-state now has to face a very different problem: how to maintain socio-cultural continuity in the face of very rapid demographic change? The way Singapore manages this challenge will have a significant impact on its political and economic future.

Singapore's population is currently estimated at 5.4 million, of which 3.3 million are citizens and 0.5 million are permanent residents (together they are called the resident population). In addition, there are 1.5 million foreigners. The problem is that the resident population has a very low fertility rate (the Total Fertility Rate (TFR) is defined as the average number of live births per woman over her lifetime). The city-state requires a TFR of 2.1 in order to keep its resident population stable, but the registered rate is 1.3, a little more than half the 'replacement rate'.

The government has long recognised the problem of low birth rates but, despite many efforts, nothing has so far succeeded in pushing up fertility. This is not a unique problem and is common to many countries in Europe and East Asia. The obvious implication is that Singapore will need to rely heavily on immigration. Note that the abysmally low TFR implies that the incumbent resident population would have to be steadily replaced by newcomers, including new citizens, merely to maintain the current population cluster. Indeed, immigration was largely responsible for the jump in population from four million in 2000 to 5.4 million today. This is not a problem in itself, since Singaporeans are generally open to immigration (after all, everyone is an immigrant within a few of generations). However, the pace of this shift has been steadily accelerating, and suddenly it has triggered a big debate on Singapore's future trajectory.

In early 2013, the government published a white paper that mentioned a population projection of 6.5–6.9 million in 2030. Although the government clarified that the projection was a guideline for infrastructure planning rather than a target, the number came under severe criticism. A part of the reaction may be due to the usual insecurities about economic competition from newcomers, but there is a deep-rooted fear about the erosion of the 'Singaporean way of life'.

Despite its bubbling ethnic mix, Singapore's economic miracle was made possible by an exceptional degree of social cohesion. At its root, many locals fear that the current pace of change may be too fast to acculturise the newcomers and maintain socio-cultural continuity. In other words, the debate over immigration in Singapore should not be trivialised as xenophobia, but must be seen as a fundamental one about the city-state's long-term viability.

One option for the city-state is to accept demographic decline and allow the population to shrink (some other Asian countries seem to be opting for this). Singapore's problem is that it is a 'global city' that requires a minimum cluster of activity. As it is, Singapore has the smallest population of any major global hub and there is a non-trivial risk that a steady decline in population would trigger a process of de-clustering. Urban history shows that once de-clustering takes place, it can gather an unstoppable momentum that is difficult to arrest (ask Detroit).

Singapore's leaders are aware of these risks and are trying hard to manage contradictory pressures. On the one hand, the pace of immigration has been slowed to what is deemed socially acceptable. On the other hand, the government has recognised that Singapore's urban mass can be increased by leveraging the hinterland. Thus, we are seeing support for urban developments in the Iskandar Development Region in Malaysia. Similarly, a high-speed rail link is being built between Singapore and Kuala Lumpur. The idea is that Singapore the city could be bigger than Singapore the country.

Such strategies may keep Singapore's economy running for a decade or two, but the country's abysmal birth rates make it inevitable that the resident population will shrink and, to some extent, be replaced by newcomers. This is why it is important that Singapore begins to think of other ways of maintaining socio-cultural continuity.

In some ways, Singapore's problem is common to all global cities where the population keeps churning. The reason that cities such as London and New York are able to maintain socio-cultural continuity despite changing demographics is that they have anchor institutions that keep the collective memory alive. Institutions that help maintain continuity in London include its universities, museums, theatres, old buildings and traditions, and even the monarchy. Cultural factors like literature too play an important role: no matter who buys/sells real estate on Baker Street, Sherlock Holmes will continue to live there. New York is similarly served by Columbia University, New York University, Central Park, Broadway, and so on.

In short, Singapore needs to make the transition from an ingenious whiz kid to a mature city with a distinct personality. This would be a big shift in the way the city-state thinks of long-term economic strategy. The good news is that the ingredients already exist for creating a distinct and lasting personality for Singapore. As a Chinese-majority city with an Indian name that started out as a European outpost in Southeast Asia, it is the meeting point of some of the world's great civilisations. In the past, this cultural mix was seen as being peripheral to Singapore's economic model, but in the long run it may prove to be its single biggest strength.

(This piece was first published in *Project Syndicate*, October 2013)

# DRAINAGE NETWORKS, NOT ROADS, ARE ARTERIES OF THE CITY

The monsoon rains have been a relief after two years of drought. However, they have also revealed that almost all Indian cities lack drainage networks. Even a modest shower will flood our roads, homes and markets, and will bring our cities to a standstill. Neglected drainage networks is not merely about the inconvenience caused by traffic jams, but is closely linked to many aspects of urban management—the spread of diseases like chikungunya and dengue and even the efficiency of public transport systems.

Ironically, the Delhi-NCR region has inherited a very extensive network of drains and canals, 'nullahs'. Architect Manit Rastogi has spent years mapping them and estimates that the network consists of 350 km of major and minor nullahs. Some of these are natural contours, but many were built as irrigation canals by medieval dynasties like the Tughlaqs. Some arterial nullahs are substantial stretches of real estate, in places 30–40 m wide. Once you notice them, you will see them everywhere—behind the prime minister's home along Race Course Road (now called Lok Kalyan Marg), past Defense Colony, through Delhi Cantonment and so on.

Unfortunately, the network suffers from complete neglect. In many places it has become a smelly sewer, in others it has been overrun by squatters. Since no one cares for them, they are easily hijacked for other purposes like car parks and roads. Municipal authorities claim that drains continue to flow under the new construction, but they are difficult to clean and get quickly clogged with garbage. It is not surprising, therefore, that even a moderate shower floods the roads.

A similar story can be told of other Indian cities: the traditional water tanks of Bengaluru, the Mithi river in Mumbai, and the Adyar catchment in Chennai. The Noyyal is marked as a perennial river in nineteenth century maps of Coimbatore, but is now a sewer. Varanasi derives its name from two streams—Varuna and Asi. The former is still a discernible river, but Asi is now a municipal drain. Many locals who live along its banks were surprised when I pointed out its course.

The maintenance of drainage networks is critical for avoiding repeated floods, but they are also a solution to another major problem faced by Indian cities—the lack of walking and cycling paths. A critical flaw in public transport systems across India is first/last mile connectivity. In all other countries, this is usually walked, but in India, one is forced to haggle with a rickshaw even for a short distance.

A nullah network, by its nature, is made of long stretches of land. In fact, for historical reasons, the nullahs usually run close to the oldest and densest neighbourhoods and are often the only open space cutting through the landscape. Rather than covering them up, walking paths should be built along the open nullahs. This would have the additional benefit of increasing public pressure to keeping the nullahs clean as people would be walking along them. Rastogi estimates that Delhi can have a first class walking/cycling network and a workable drainage network for a fraction of the money being currently spent on large, centralised sewage treatment plants.

The dual use of water networks as walking paths is not uncommon across the world. Many Western cities use paths along water-bodies as walkways and several Asian cities have adopted this model in recent years.

Till the 1970s, Singapore river was a foul-smelling stream that took in industrial discharge as well as waste from hawkers and squatters. In 1977, Prime Minister Lee Kuan Yew put a target that it would be possible to eat fish from the river in ten years' time. Over the next few years, thousands of hawkers and squatters were relocated while industrial discharge was diverted to sewage treatment plants. By 1984, the river was clean enough for the government to organise a 'mass-swim' that included senior government officials. Today, the old riverside warehouses of Boat Quay and Clarke Quay are among the most visited tourist sites in Asia.

The Cheonggyecheon stream in Seoul is another example of watershed restoration as urban renewal strategy. In the 1950s, the stream had become a smelly drain carrying industrial and household sewage. An elevated highway was built over it in 1968. However, in 2003, the local mayor decided to pull down the highway and restore seven km of the stream. The stretch is now the centerpiece of the city and 80,000 people use it every day.

In an automobile obsessed age, we think of roads as the arteries of the city, but it is really drainage networks that should play this part. They are not merely to ensure that roads do not get flooded after a downpour, but are an organic part of the city as green lungs, water-table recharge, public transport, waste management, and spaces for leisure. Other Asian cities have come to recognise this in recent years and it is time we did too.

(This piece was originally published in *Hindustan Times*, September 2016)

# THE SPLINTERED DEMOCRACY

Indian cities clearly should be managed better. Mega-cities like Mumbai may blame the sheer size of population and migration, but India's small towns are no better managed. If anything, small towns in the Gangetic plains are even worse managed than the big metropolitan cities. We cannot even blame poverty. There are other countries—like Vietnam—which are both very poor and very densely populated, but do not suffer from the squalor that one associates with urban India. In short, there are no excuses for poor urban governance.

It has long been argued that the solution lies in decentralisation. Issues like waste management and water supply are local issues and need to be resolved locally. Fair enough. The newly built city of Gurugram is expected to have an elected municipal government by the end of the year. In theory, this will allow municipal issues to be tackled locally rather than in faraway Chandigarh, the state capital. As a resident of the town, I should be jumping with joy but, like most others, I am ambivalent. The reason is that local municipal government has not been a great success anywhere in India. What is the problem?

## THE HISTORICAL BACKGROUND

In pre-colonial times, city government was handled by the local ruler or Mughal governor. This was an ad hoc system that the British attempted to modernise and institutionalise. In 1882, Lord Ripon created laws covering the establishment of local bodies, their powers and financial arrangements. This led to the evolution of municipal bodies in at least some towns. Unlike later, local bodies attracted leading citizens and politicians. Calcutta Municipal Corporation, for instance, had well-known people like Subhas Bose as chief executive officer and later as mayor.

When India became independent, it was envisaged that the government would have a decentralised structure with three tiers. In practice, however, the political dominance of a single party combined with socialist planning led to a very centralised power structure. Even when power did devolve to the states, it seldom percolated to the local bodies. In fact, state governments—usually dominated by rural politicians— saw municipal bodies as a threat and actively limited them. An attempt was made to force decentralisation in 1992 through the 74th amendment to the Constitution. Two decades later, municipal bodies remain very weak—their finances are poor and their powers unclear. Not surprisingly, citizens are usually apathetic to local body elections.

# RWA DEMOCRACY

Apathy towards local government does not mean that citizens do not care about local issues. Quite to the contrary, they actively participate in groups like Resident Welfare Associations (RWAs) created under legal provisions such as the Apartment Ownership Act (most states have their own version).

Neighbourhood RWAs have long existed in different forms in Delhi's 'colonies' or in the apartment blocks of Mumbai and Kolkata. They tended to limit themselves to micro-issues related to building maintenance. However, they are becoming increasingly vocal platforms because of the failure of the wider system.

The new-style RWAs are most active in new townships like Gurugram that have mushroomed in the last decade. Typically, there is no pre-exiting elected body in these areas and the RWAs are the only form of local representation. However, both urban infrastructure and RWAs are organised according to 'colonies'. Urban governance, therefore, is splintering up into a series of gated communities. This is even true of the poor who live in 'urban villages' that also organise themselves internally. There is no direct link between this inward-looking arrangement and the governance of the overall city.

As India experiences rapid urban growth, this phenomenon will become even more widespread. Note that many of the new RWAs represent very large areas and tens of thousands of residents. Increasingly, RWAs are taking on powerful political interests and real estate developers. However, all this is happening through agitation rather than the governance system.

## UNIFYING PARALLEL SYSTEMS

Interestingly, RWAs represent a form of citizen participation that involves the middle class that has been usually apathetic to mainstream politics for many decades. The political class has begun to take note of this change. A few years ago, the then Delhi Chief Minister Sheila Dikshit introduced a scheme called bhagidari to tap into the energies of the RWA movement to help solve local issues.

Unfortunately, the RWA-based 'democracy' is far from perfect. There is a great deal of internal politics and sometimes we have parallel RWAs representing the same area. Very often, they look at issues from the narrow view of their community rather than that of the wider urban fabric. The needs of the poor are frequently ignored as they are not property owners and consequently not RWA members. However, the biggest problem is that the RWA system does not fit easily into the constitutionally mandated system of wards and local bodies. This is why the bhagidari experiment has yielded mixed results at best. In effect, we have two parallel legal frameworks—one for the municipal corporation and one for the RWA. In Delhi, this is further complicated by the fact that both the state and Central governments are actively involved in municipal affairs.

The first step towards better municipal governance would

be to synchronise the two systems so that local democracy is unified. One way could be that RWA representatives are made part of the municipal council. This may not however be straightforward. Local body elections are based on the principle of 'one vote per person', whereas RWAs are based on real estate ownership. Nonetheless, we need to find a way in which all interests are reasonably represented within a unified framework. If not, we will continue with the current system of splintered democracy.

(This piece was originally published in *Business Standard*, March 2010)

# ECONOMICS

Economics is the field that perhaps has the most to gain from the insights of the CAS framework, but this is also where it will face the greatest resistance from entrenched orthodoxy. So much has been invested by the academic and policy establishment in Newtonian models that even those who acknowledge their repeated failures, will fall back on them in practice to make grand predictions about the future (note that I have no problem using such models for stress-testing and simple scenario analysis, but that is another story).

The first essay in this section lays out some of the basic principles of CAS as applied to economics and emphasises the importance of flexibility, transparency and feedback loops. Readers familiar with the Austrian school of economics will see its influence in many of the essays. Whether Schumpeter's creative destruction or Hayek's price discovery, the approach is based on the idea that we live in an ever-changing, unstable world where individuals and governments have limited ability to predict or optimise the economy. The parallels to the CAS approach should be obvious.

Contrary to popular perception, the Austrian school is not

a narrow argument for minimum government libertarianism. It is a framework of thinking that lends itself to a surprisingly broad range, albeit always retaining a suspicion of unrestrained statism. In this section, the reader will find CAS and Austrian school ideas brushing shoulders with those of Kautilya, the fourth century political-economist, who also co-founded the Mauryan empire. Kautilya was no libertarian and the *Arthashastra* (the treatise on Wealth) makes no bones about the need for a strong State. However, his approach is based on two pillars—the rule of law and the need for restraint.

Interestingly, his argument for restraining the State is not based so much on concerns about human rights and freedom (the usual Western approach) but derived from a deep suspicion of civil servants whom he considers inherently corrupt! My hope is to provide the reader with a sense of wide-ranging ideas that influence my thinking on economics and governance.

For all my suspicion of single-point forecasting and overly prescriptive worldviews, I recognise that forethought is essential—and that it should be influenced by hard evidence before theory (although the latter matters too). In particular, there is value in studying long-range historical experience as a guide to the future. As the saying goes, history does not repeat itself, but it often rhymes. Hence the collection includes many musings about the future: whether or not the US dollar can be replaced; Trump's economic policies; the impact of future Chinese deleveraging and trends in population growth. Many of these pieces were written some years ago but I have not updated them so that readers can look at how events actually panned out compared to how I was thinking at that time.

As I had argued back in 2011, the US dollar remains the world's anchor currency and is in no danger of being replaced by the Euro or the Yuan as some analysts had predicted back then. Similarly, growing evidence supports my decades-old view that the collapse of fertility will slow down world population growth much sooner than expected by most demographers (including the UN population Division). On the other hand, my view that large-scale Chinese deleveraging would deluge the world with cheap capital is yet to come true (there is plenty of Chinese capital about, but not yet in the scales I had been predicting). As it turned out, President Trump did opt for expansionary economic policies that generated strong growth, but he has so far relied more on tax cuts than the infrastructure build out that I had expected in 2016. But then, CAS practitioners are satisfied by being roughly right and avoiding being precisely wrong.

# THE END OF EQUILIBRIUM ECONOMICS?

It is more than eight years since the beginning of the global financial crisis. Although the world economy came back from the abyss, it never fully recovered. Now, latest data from across the world suggests that we may be tethering at the edge of another downturn. So why have negative interest rates, and waves of central bank liquidity failed to restore sustained growth or trigger inflation?

There are a number of interrelated factors that have been blamed: excess capacity, savings glut, demographics, indebtedness and so on. However, a large part of the blame must lie with policymakers and professional economists who have systematically failed to anticipate breakdowns but continue to advocate measures that have already been proved ineffective.

They seem to think that if zero interest rates did not work, then surely negative rates will do the job. So why are so many well-trained professionals unable to solve the problem? The reality is that mainstream economics is a dead horse and there is no point in flogging it. Most conventional frameworks from Keynesian to Monetarist tend to think of economies as Victorian steam engines where an optimal 'equilibrium' can be attained by pulling the right levers and pulleys, and shovelling more coal into the furnace.

This line of thinking inevitably manifests itself in large-scale Computable General Equilibrium (CGE) models. Almost all policymaking institutions spend enormous resources building them. This is inexplicable given that CGE models have never been able to predict a major economic event. The problem is that economies are not Victorian machines and no amount of refining the CGE framework will get us better results.

## THE DOG AND THE FRISBEE

An alternative framework is to rethink economies as Complex Adaptive Systems, which are made up of large numbers of independent agents that are constantly interacting with each other and evolving. Examples include ecological systems, cities, financial markets, the English language and, arguably, Hinduism. Note that CAS's do not follow the Newtonian logic of CGE and have no inherent tendency to gravitate to a stable equilibrium. They also suffer from the Law of Unintended Consequences and can respond to the same stimulus in multiple ways. This means that managing such systems is less about pre-planning and more about constant monitoring, feedback and flexible adjustment.

Let me contrast the CAS and CGE frameworks through

an example popularised by Andrew Haldane of the Bank of England. Say, a man is throwing a Frisbee for his dog to catch. If the dog was a CGE proponent, it would model the shape of the Frisbee, the man's muscle strength, wind speed, gravity and so on. Even if the dog is a genius, however, it would probably still fail to catch the Frisbee because there are just too many moving parts to model.

In reality, the average dog has no problem catching the Frisbee because all it does is closely watch the flying object and constantly adjust its own position, i.e., monitor, feedback, adapt. This is the CAS approach.

## TRANSPARENCY AND FLEXIBILITY

So, how would this apply to the current economic predicament? First of all, let us be clear that there is no such thing as an 'equilibrium' growth rate to which the world economy naturally gravitates. Similarly, all periods of economic growth in history have been accompanied by large global imbalances. A return to so-called balance is not obviously a good thing. There is also no 'neutral' or 'natural' interest rate to which the US Federal Reserve needs reverting. So, the Fed should act on the best available data and not be swayed by some preconceived notion of normality.

Second, it is far from obvious that even 'helicopter money' would revive demand. Recipients of such cash injections are just as likely to save it as spend it (especially when deflation is increasing the value of cash holdings).

Instead, the increase in the central bank's liabilities

could have many unintended consequences that could come back to bite at an inconvenient time in the future. Third, central banks and other regulators need to take a very different approach towards regulating the financial system. Conventional thinking is that increasing regulation always reduces the vulnerability to crises. However, banks were heavily regulated even before 2007 and that did not prevent the crisis.

Why should ever more regulations help? The imposition of increasingly cumbersome rules is making financial systems inflexible and less transparent. The CAS approach would suggest that this makes the banking system more vulnerable, not less.

Indeed, the new complicated Basel-related regulations are likely to have unintended consequences that may cause the next crisis. It's better to have simple regulations combined with active supervision. Policymakers must realise that regulation and supervision are different things, and there is a trade-off between them. To conclude, the key implication of the CAS framework is that a complex world cannot be managed by increasing complexity but through simplicity and flexibility. Since there is no equilibrium, it's all about triggering virtuous cycles and then managing the distortions that necessarily accompany them.

(This piece was originally published in *The Economic Times*, March 2016)

# AT SIXTY–RETHINKING THE INDIAN STATE

It is now sixty years since we became a Republic and the Indian State came into being. Yet, each passing day brings fresh evidence of the State's inability to respond to threats to its citizens: witness the daily Naxalite attacks in eastern India, jehadi terror from Mumbai to Kashmir, the parole for Manu Sharma, the rampant poaching of tigers, and our apologetic response to Chinese pressure on Arunachal. These are not mundane failures in the provision of public services but go to the heart of what we should expect of the Indian State.

## BACK TO THE BASICS

We tend to expect a lot of things from the State—from defence of our borders to clearance of garbage. We also expect it to actively promote economic development and a myriad of other social objectives. Therefore, we have given the State very wide-ranging powers. However, the

Indian State is clearly unable to deliver on most of these expectations. Instead, we have ended up with a weak but all-pervasive State that does not have a clear set of priorities. Since it does not have a clear set of priorities, we cannot judge its performance and hold it accountable. What is worse is that unscrupulous individuals have been able to subvert the powers of the State to serve their own ends.

The first thing we need to do is to decide what is the most important role of the State. Robert Nozick, one of twentieth century's most influential political philosophers, was of the opinion that the first responsibility of the State is to protect its citizens against violence, theft and fraud as well as to enforce contracts. Indeed, Max Weber defined the State as the apparatus that has the monopoly over the use of force in a given territory. A State that cannot enforce this monopoly is not a State at all.

This echoes the traditional Indian notion of the state. According to Kautilya's *Arthashastra,* the maintenance of law and order and the dispensation of justice is the science of government. Similarly, as Gurcharan Das has argued in his latest book, the one thing that the Kurukshetra War teaches us is that there will always be individuals like Duryodhana and society needs to curb them with force, if necessary. Being 'good' like Yudhishthir, is not the State's first mandate.

Contrast this with the bewildering responsibilities that we have burdened the modern Indian State with. I am not arguing that the government should abandon all other responsibilities, but merely pointing out that the maintenance of law and order and dispensation of justice (including enforcement of contracts and the protection of property rights) must be the starting point. Today's Indian State fails miserably at this basic responsibility—witness the moribund legal system, and the usurpation of power by non-State actors like the Naxalites.

In short, I am arguing that the Indian State must be strong and it must restore its monopoly over the use of force. This includes the urgent reform of the police, legal system and the administrative apparatus. This is far more important for the country's economic and social future than spending on various government 'development' schemes. As the *Arthashastra* puts it, 'Progress in this world depends on governance and on the maintenance of order.'

A strong State is not without its own dangers as there is always a risk that it may become totalitarian (we experienced this ourselves during the Emergency). This is why other democracies have put serious limits on the powers of the State. The need to limit the powers of the monarch (i.e., the State) has been an important aspect of the development of British democracy since the Magna Carta. The Magna Carta Libertatum, signed in 1215 AD, literally means 'The Great Charter of Freedoms'. Similarly, the Tenth Amendment of the US Constitution ensures that powers that have not been explicitly granted to the federal government will continue to reside with the people.

India took many things from the British and American constitutions, but there is a general assumption that the rights of the people need not be defended against a benign State. Thus, the 'benign' State is allowed to interfere with all aspects of the nation's life and individuals are expected to fall in line for the greater good. The most obvious manifestation of this phenomenon was the attempt to accelerate economic development through socialist planning and industrial licensing. However, this attitude is evident in all aspects of public policy. Till 2001, the citizens of India were not officially allowed to unfurl the national flag—even this was the prerogative of the State.

Although industrial licensing was abolished after the crisis of 1991, the overall statist framework remains in place. This provides ample scope for corruption and misuse. Virtually no Indian trusts the country's politicians and civil servants. Why then do we give them so many powers that are not essential to general governance?

## THE 'STRONG' BUT 'LIMITED' STATE

The limited State should focus on two broad areas. First, it should focus on framework issues like defence, internal security, policing, justice, foreign policy, monetary policy, financial regulation and so on. Second, it should provide for public goods where market-solutions will clearly not work—environmental protection, public health, and so on. The Indian State should be encouraged to make sure that it does a good job of these before it attempts anything else.

There is often a presumption that a limited State that focuses on institutions of governance is somehow less concerned about the welfare of the common citizen than the interventionist State. In turn, this flows from a belief that the enforcement of contracts and property rights mainly benefits the rich. Nothing can be further from reality. The rich and powerful will always find ways to protect their interests (as Manu Sharma's 'parole' clearly demonstrated). The properly functioning legal framework is mainly in the interest of the poor and weak. This is not a new thought.

In the *Arthashastra,* Kautilya points that the failure to provide justice leads to matsya nyaya—the Law of the Fish where the big fish swallow the small.

Kautilya's vision has a great deal of relevance even today. For instance, take the Naxalite insurrection in eastern India. Conventional wisdom is that this is due to the lack of jobs and the so-called 'development'. In reality, it is about property rights and the exploitation of the region's natural resources with the active connivance of the State (and the cynical manipulation of resentments by non-State actors). In Nandigram, the local people were not asking for jobs and government schemes. They merely did not want to sell their land to a government that was arbitrarily using its powers of eminent domain. As can be seen, the solution for India's current problems does not lie in the welfare schemes of a weak and all-pervasive State. It lies in a State that zealously guards its monopoly over the use of force in its territory but at the same time, is limited in how it can intervene in the lives of its citizens.

(This piece was originally published in *Business Standard,* January 2010)

# 25 YEARS OF REFORMS: WHY 1991 IS A TURNING POINT OF SIMILAR IMPORTANCE AS 1947

It is likely that future Indian schoolchildren will be made to learn two important dates from the twentieth century: 1947 and 1991. The importance of 1947 is obvious, but why is 1991 a turning point of similar importance?

One could argue that 1947 saw political power shift from a foreign-born elite to an Indian-born elite. This was undoubtedly an important change, but it carried forward a top-down mindset that a tiny group of 'wise men' knew what was best for the rest of the population. This thinking was embodied in every level of national life—economic, social and cultural.

Thus, a tiny group of planners led by P.C. Mahalanobis could decide how to allocate all economic resources. A handful of business conglomerates cornered all industrial licences. Encouraged by the thinking of Le Corbusier, urban planners could encode rigid master plans that decided how people led their lives into perpetuity. A small clique of intellectuals and editors, supported by State-controlled media and academia, could tell people what to think.

For all the socialist rhetoric, this system perpetuated the power of a small elite—political dynasties, business dynasties, even entertainment dynasties flourished. It should be no surprise that with the exception of the Ambanis, the top business families of the 1990s were the same as those of the 1940s.

Defenders of Nehru will argue that the failures of the system were not apparent for decades. Far from it. The term 'License Raj' was coined in the 1950s by C. Rajagopalachari, who predicted the corruption and inefficiency that was to follow. Life Insurance Corporation was nationalised in 1956 and within months, its resources were being plundered by politically linked groups. This resulted in the Mundhra Scandal of 1958 that was exposed by Feroze Gandhi. Rather than acknowledge the problem, Jawaharlal Nehru cut off links with his son-in-law.

It was more than obvious by the 1970s that the Nehruvian model had failed. However, establishment economist Raj Krishna cynically dubbed the poor economic performance as the 'Hindu rate of growth'. In other words, India's cultural and religious traditions were at fault and not economic policies. India had failed Nehru and not the other way around.

Enormous resources were used to bolster intellectual justification for the failing system. Institutions like the

Jawaharlal Nehru University were created explicitly for this purpose and an elaborate system of national awards and positions was built to promote loyalists at public expense.

Thus, when reforms finally came in 1991, it was due to economic collapse and not a change in mindset. With a few notable exceptions, the leading Indian intellectuals of that time were unanimous that liberalisation was a bad thing.

So, when Finance Minister Manmohan Singh presented the Budget in February 1992, he felt it was necessary to say, 'Our nation will remain eternally grateful to Jawaharlal Nehru for his vision....' He concluded the speech with, 'Tonight I feel like I am going to the theatre. Let the assassins be informed, I am prepared for the onslaught.'

Only when one re-reads these words that one recognises the political risks Prime Minister Narasimha Rao was taking by liberalising the economy. He was not just unwinding industrial licensing, but a quasi-feudal oligarchy that pervaded every sphere of life in India—a process that is still not complete.

It is now twenty-seven years since the liberalisation process was initiated. New business leaders, writers, sports stars, and more broadly a new middle class has emerged who are not beholden to public sector largesse. What is extraordinary is that despite obvious improvement in economic and social indicators, reformers still struggle to make a case for basic changes.

The reason for this is that the intellectual and institutional framework of the Nehruvian project was not systematically replaced. Academia remains in the firm grip of the old mindset. It was only in 2014 that the Planning Commission was finally abolished.

Although remnants of the Nehruvian apparatus need to be unwound, the next twenty-five years should focus on building a new system. The alternative to the top-down, all-pervasive Nehruvian State is not necessarily a minimalist, libertarian one. India needs a strong but limited State that focuses on creating an open framework that allows bottom-up innovation, risk-taking and social mobility.

The creation of such a State still needs political leadership, but one that addresses framework issues: basic infrastructure, internal/external security, simple tax system and so on. Most importantly, the State must be able to enforce laws and contracts.

A bottom-up economic and social structure is all about how various entities interact independently with each other. Such a system cannot function with thirty-four million cases stuck in courts. This is why the next generation of reforms must be about transparent laws, quick judicial process and reliable policing.

Just as 1947 gave us independence from colonial rule, 1991 started the process that gave Indians freedom from a self-defeating mindset. The next big turning point in Indian history will be the year when we finally get serious about reforming the legal system. I hope 2017 will be that year.

(This piece was originally published in *The Economic Times*, July 2016)

# MOVING THE BEHEMOTH

India's growth acceleration is now visible to all. The key challenge is to make it sustainable. This requires invigoration of reforms. For this, the Prime Minister and Finance Minister have recently called for 'political space'. But we also need a sound strategy to generate political support to intensify the reforms. At this stage of the political cycle, legal reforms will not only generate a large political consensus, but will be quick-yielding in terms of accelerating growth and making it more inclusive.

India still has infrastructural weaknesses such as potholed roads, power brownouts and over-crowded trains that had plagued it in the pre-liberalisation era. Yet, there is no doubt that many parts of the economy have been completely transformed in the last fifteen years. Why have some segments changed so dramatically while others have languished? In order to understand the phenomenon, it is instructive to look at those areas that have been at the forefront of the country's new success.

India's financial markets have been dramatically transformed over the last decade. Not so long ago, these markets were bogged down by illiquid instruments, opaque practices and frequent financial scandals. In contrast, the country's capital markets are now considered to be among the most transparent and well-regulated in the world. This improvement has been rewarded with sharply higher asset prices and improved liquidity.

What caused this change? In a word—governance. This term relates to both the quality of 'rules' that govern market participants as well as the 'enforcement' of rules. In the case of India's financial markets, the change has been made possible because of improved governance by the relevant institutions—SEBI, Reserve Bank of India, NSE and so on. In turn, this has had huge multiplier effects on the economy as a whole through improvements in resource allocation, corporate governance and returns to investors.

However, this same principle applies to the economic system in general. Good governance is a precondition for success, especially in a liberalised economy where markets are harnessed to promote better allocation of resources and equitable outcomes. Legal infrastructure is the key institutional framework through which the State provides good governance. The legal system incorporates both the rules of engagement (laws and regulations) as well as the enforcement of these rules via the police and the judiciary.

Furthermore, it should be recognised that the legal infrastructure can be an agent of change in common-law countries like India. This is a role that is most often ignored by economists because the legal system is seen merely as the blind and passive enforcement of a static body of rules. However, in the British common-law tradition—India firmly belongs to this camp—each judgement creates a precedent that can be used in future cases. In other words, a good judicial system can be an active agent of change, rather than just a passive enforcer.

As every Indian knows, two things are necessary for a good game of cricket—a set of consistent rules that are understood by everyone, and even-handed enforcement, viz., good umpires. This is also true for the economic game. Unfortunately, the Indian legal system fails on both counts.

India has a very large body of laws and regulations—national laws, state laws, municipal laws and administrative directives, among many others. Unfortunately, there is little harmony, consistency or inter-linkage of the laws. Many laws date back to the nineteenth century and still provide the legal framework for activities that were never imagined at that time. Some areas are absurdly over-regulated while others do not have meaningful laws.

For instance, there are almost fifty labour-related laws at the national level alone, together with associated rules and regulations. In addition to these Central labour laws, there is a plethora of state level laws and administrative directives. On top of these, there are several state and Central laws that indirectly affect labour. The content of these laws is, of course, another matter—a large area of debate in its own right. But this is a pointer to the sheer complexity of the legal framework related to the simple, routine act of employing workers.

Not surprisingly, such a confusing body of law makes it difficult for everyone to understand the rules of engagement. Even if a person were diligently law-abiding, it would be virtually impossible for that person to function without knowingly or unknowingly breaking some rule or the other. Indeed, much of the booming call centre outsourcing business is technically illegal, according to some state laws. In 2005, the Labour Ministry of the Haryana government invoked Section 30 of the Punjab Shops and Commercial Establishments Act, 1958, to disallow women from working night shifts at call centres in Gurugram.

There are even greater problems with enforcement. The Indian judicial system is infamous for the slow pace of processing even the most routine of cases. As a result, there are over thirty million cases pending in the courts. This does not include the large number of cases stuck in various tribunals and quasi-judicial bodies.

It is not just delays that are a concern but also the systematic failure to deliver justice, especially in the criminal justice system. It is common knowledge that two-thirds of jail inmates are undertrials who are being forced to live in jail as they cannot afford bail or do not have the legal support to apply for it. Many of these prisoners have been in jail for years without coming to trial—some have long exceeded the maximum sentences for their alleged crimes. At the same time, the judicial system seems unable to identify and punish genuine offenders. The conviction rate, apparently, is less than five per cent.

Given all these issues, it should be no surprise that one should wish for reforms in the legal system. Unfortunately, legal reform is usually seen as peripheral to the economic reform process.

However, it is the single-most important reform initiative for improving governance. This is the one thing that will have a dramatic multiplier effect through the entire economy. Of particular interest is the possibility of using the judicial system, combined with the Right to Information (RTI) Act, to improve the provision of public goods and services.

What makes it even more attractive is that it is unlikely to require a great deal of additional public expenditure. A large proportion of cases involve the government on both sides—these should simply be resolved internally through administrative measures. For the rest, efficiency can be drastically improved by increased investment in this sector. No formal estimates are available of how much money is required to set the judicial system right. But preliminary estimates suggest that to stabilise the judicial backlog at current levels, together with significant quality improvements, an additional allocation of about Rs 4,000 crores fixed investment and around Rs 2,000 crores as annual recurring costs will be required.

The potential gains to the economy will be multiples of these expenditures. Finally, perhaps, the most important reason for focusing on legal reforms at this stage is that these can receive bipartisan support as everyone gains from them. There are no losers here and the results will be quick.

(This piece was originally published in *Hindustan Times*, October 2006, and is credited to the author and Vijay Kelkar, former Finance Secretary, Government of India & former Chairman, Finance Commission)

# WHY INDIA NEED TO NO LONGER BE AN ASHOKAN REPUBLIC, BUT A CHANAKYAN ONE

Our Republic was established on this day in 1950. So, it is a good day to re-evaluate the nature of the Indian State. One approach would be to compare it to what the framers of the Constitution had envisioned. Another, to contrast it with developments in other countries. But what if we compared it to the thoughts of Kautilya, one of the greatest political thinkers India has ever produced?

Kautilya, also called Chanakya, is often called India's Machiavelli. But this colonial-era epithet is grossly unfair. For all his fame, Niccolò Machiavelli was a small-time political adviser in Florence who was ousted by his rivals. In contrast, Kautilya was the co-founder of one of the largest empires of the ancient world.

More importantly, for our purposes, Machiavelli's writings are narrowly about how to how capture and maintain power using unscrupulous means. In contrast, the focus of Kautilya's *Arthashastra* (the treatise on Wealth) is on governance. There is occasional mention of intrigue and spies, but only in the wider context of maintaining order. Most of the book is about taxation, municipal laws, the legal system, property rights, labour laws and so on.

Many of the specific measures suggested by Kautilya are influenced by the technology and social mores of his times. But we can certainly apply his principles to the Indian republic. Conveniently, the *Arthashastra* explicitly lays out the principles in several instances.

The text is clear that the single most important role of the state is to avoid matsya nyaya—the Law of the Fish—where the big fish consume the small. This means that, before it does anything else, the State must ensure defence, internal security, rule of law and, most importantly, have complete monopoly over violence within its territory.

Notice how the *Arthashastra* is not about welfare schemes of a nanny State. Instead, it contains long discussions on property rights, enforcement of contracts and consumer protection. Kautilya is clearly wary of government officials, for, he says, 'Just as it is impossible to know when a fish is drinking water, so it is impossible to tell when government officials misappropriate money.'

This is not to suggest that Kautilya was an early libertarian arguing for minimalist government. Far from it. He advocated a government that actively provided public goods, regulated markets and encouraged public sector undertakings in areas like mining. The emphasis, however, is always on maintaining the overall framework of governance rather than on specific interventions in people's lives. The text repeatedly states that self-restraint is the single most important attribute in a king. In other words, the Kautilyan ideal is a 'strong' but 'limited' State.

The idea can be illustrated by what Kautilya would have had to say about today's debates on prohibition of alcohol or the Supreme Court ban on jallikattu, the traditional Tamil sport of bull-taming, 'People taking to pleasures consume little; they do so to relax from the fatigue of work and get back to work again after relaxation. A decadent king, on the other hand, oppresses the people....'

This statement does not mean that Kautilya didn't care for animal welfare or drunkards' disorderly behaviour. But his approach would have been to allow most activities as long as they remained within a framework of rules about health and safety.

Moreover, he was far more concerned about restraining the misuse of State power in everyday life than in banning the so-called vices. Thus, prostitution is considered a legal but regulated profession. Kautilya writes that 'proper procedure must be used to induct the virgin daughter of a prostitute, whether willing or not; coercive methods shall not be used.'

So what would Kautilya do if he were alive today? A reading of the *Arthashastra* suggests that the first thing he would do is fix the judicial system. He would look on the thirty-two million pending cases as the epitome of matsanyaya. Kautilya's thinking would be that the delivery of justice is more important for the welfare of the poor than any subsidy scheme.

Second, he would invest heavily in internal security to sternly put down violence from terrorists, Maoists, criminals and mobs of various shades. Many social scientists today take the view that poverty and inequality lead to social disorder. But Kautilya would argue that the direction of causality runs in reverse.

Third, he would attempt a dramatic simplification of taxes, regulations and the administrative structure. His view would be that every complication breeds corruption.

There is a stark contrast between the above approach and the paternalistic thinking of Emperor Ashoka just two generations later. In his inscriptions, Ashoka repeatedly says that he considers his subjects as his children and then states that his officials are like nannies meant to look after them.

He then goes on to announce all kinds of restrictions on what people can eat or do on certain days. 'On the three Chaturmasis, the three days of Tisa and the 14th and 15th of Uposatha, fish are protected and not to be sold. On the eighth of every fortnight, on the 14th and 15th, on Tisa, Punarvasu, the three Chaturmasis and other auspicious days, bulls are not to be castrated....' A special cadre of officials called dhamma mahammatas—religious police—were given the task of enforcing these laws.

The over-extended Ashokan state caused the Mauryan empire to disintegrate from rebellion and fiscal stress while the emperor was still alive. Yet, the dominance of Nehruvian thinking in the twentieth century led the Indian republic to follow the Ashokan model for the last sixty-six years. The result is a weak and all-pervasive State. Perhaps it is time to revisit Kautilya. After all, it was he who created a large, well-functioning empire, while Ashoka presided over its disintegration.

(This piece was originally published in *The Economic Times*, January 2016)

# 'DEMOGRAPHIC DIVIDEND' IS UNDER WAY WITH COLLAPSE IN FERTILITY

Latest survey data suggest that Indian fertility has fallen sharply in recent years and is already at the 'replacement level' needed to keep the population stable. Urban fertility is now at levels seen in developed countries and in some places among the lowest in the world.

These readings suggest a big change in India's demographic trajectory. It also adds to the likelihood that world population will peak a lot sooner than is widely believed.

According to recently released Sample Registration System data, the country's Total Fertility Rate (TFR) stood at 2.3 in 2013. TFR is the average number of children per woman if she lives to the end of her child-bearing years. In developed countries, a TFR of 2.1 is required in order to keep the population stable (ignoring migration). In India, this is around 2.3 due to higher infant mortality and a skewed gender ratio. In other words, the country's TFR is already at the 'replacement rate'.

The TFR for rural areas stands at 2.5, but that for urban India is down at 1.8—marginally below the readings for Britain and the US. An important implication of this is that India's overall TFR will almost certainly fall below replacement as it rapidly urbanises over the next twenty years.

There continues to be wide variations in the fertility rates across the country. Readings for the southern states have been low for some time, but are now dropping sharply in many northern states.

Tamil Nadu has a TFR of 1.7, but so do Punjab, Himachal Pradesh and Delhi. Uttar Pradesh and Bihar continue to have the country's highest TFR at 3.1 and 3.5 respectively, but these are also falling steadily.

## DEMISE OF THE BHADRALOK

Interestingly, West Bengal has the lowest fertility in the country with a TFR reading of 1.6. The level for rural Bengal is 1.8, but is a shockingly low 1.2 for the cities. This is one of the lowest levels in the world and is at par with Singapore and South Korea.

One can see this even more clearly when one compares the birth rates across major Indian cities (The birth rate is the number of live births per thousand population.) Kolkata had a birth rate of just 9.9 over 2011–13 compared to 15.1for Chennai, 17.8 for Delhi and 14.7 for Mumbai.

Separate data has not been published for Kolkata's educated middle class—the 'bhadralok' class. However, fertility tends to fall with higher education across India and it is fair to presume that the number for the bhadralok class would be even lower than for the overall city.

This is in addition to large-scale outward migration of Kolkata's educated youth in recent decades to Bengaluru, Delhi-NCR and across the world. If these trends continue, the traditional Bengali bhadralok class will go almost extinct within a generation in its city of origin. Of course, a new middle class will rise to take its place, but this will have important cultural and political implications. Other Indian cities too are witnessing the rise of a new middle class. But in their case, it is driven more by upward mobility and inward migration rather than the rapid demise of the old middle class.

## END OF POPULATION GROWTH

The fall in fertility below replacement levels does not mean that population growth will immediately stop. Indians are living longer.

So, for another twenty-five plus years, falling death rates will compensate for falling birth rates. Nonetheless, the latest survey results will hopefully change the minds of those under the impression that Indian population would remain young and keep growing forever. The 'demographic dividend' phase is already underway and will last just one generation.

The trends in fertility have important implications for policy. First, social policy must shift focus from birth control to other issues like infant mortality. Second, long-term schemes like pension systems must anticipate a time when the old population will be expanding much faster than the youth population.

Third, the provision of education, health and other services needs to prepare for the demographic turn. Population structure may appear to change slowly. But, as Japan and China have discovered, it is a powerful dynamic once it gathers pace. Indeed, some Indian states will need to face these issues within a decade.

The fall in Indian fertility is not unique. It is in line with what every other country has experienced at a certain economic stage. Developed countries have been below replacement rates for decades now. But fertility is now plunging across emerging markets. China, Brazil and Russia are all below replacement level. Only Africa still has very high birth rate, but this too will fall eventually.

This is why most world population forecasts are flawed. The United Nations predicts that world population will rise from the current 7.3 billion to 11.2 billion by the end of the century. However, fertility trends suggest that it will peak at a much lower level (perhaps closer to nine billion) before declining. One could argue that this would be a good thing. But a shrinking, ageing population will bring its own challenges.

(This piece was originally published in *The Economic Times*, May 2016)

# THE END OF POPULATION GROWTH

According to the United Nations' Population Division, the world's human population hit seven billion on 31 October. As always happens whenever we approach such a milestone, this one has produced a spike in conferences, seminars, and learned articles, including the usual dire Malthusian predictions. After all, the UN forecasts that world population will rise to 9.3 billion in 2050 and surpass ten billion by the end of this century.

Such forecasts, however, misrepresent underlying demographic dynamics. The future we face is not one of too much population growth, but too little.

Most countries conducted their national population census last year, and the data suggest that fertility rates are plunging in most of them. Birth rates have been low in developed countries for some time, but now they are falling rapidly in the majority of developing countries. Chinese, Russians, and Brazilians are no longer replacing themselves, while Indians are having far fewer children. Indeed, global fertility will fall to the replacement rate in a little more than a decade. Population may keep growing until mid-century, owing to rising longevity, but, reproductively speaking, our species should no longer be expanding.

What demographers call the Total Fertility Rate is the average number of live births per woman over her lifetime. In the long run, a population is said to be stable if the TFR is at the replacement rate, which is a little above 2.3 for the world as a whole, and somewhat lower, at 2.1, for developed countries, reflecting their lower infant-mortality rates.

The TFR for most developed countries now stands well below replacement levels. The OECD (Organisation for Economic Cooperation and Development) average is at around 1.74, but some countries, including Germany and Japan, produce less than 1.4 children per woman. However, the biggest TFR declines in recent years have been in developing countries. The TFR in China and India was 6.1 and 5.9, respectively, in 1950. It now stands at 1.8 in China, owing to the authorities' aggressive one-child policy, while rapid urbanisation and changing social attitudes have brought down India's TFR to 2.6.

An additional factor could depress future birth rates in China and India. The Chinese census suggests that there are 118.6 boys being born for every 100 girls. Similarly, India has a gender ratio at birth of around 110 boys for every 100 girls, with large regional variations. Compare this to the natural ratio of 105 boys per 100 girls. The deviation is usually attributed to a cultural preference for boys, which will take an additional toll on both populations, as the future scarcity of women implies that both countries' effective reproductive capacity is below what is suggested by the unadjusted TFR.

Indeed, after adjusting for the gender imbalance, China's Effective Fertility Rate (EFR) is around 1.5, and India's is 2.45. In other words, the Chinese are very far from replacing themselves, and the Indians are only slightly above the replacement rate. The EFR stands at around 2.4 for the world as a whole, barely above the replacement rate. Current trends suggest that the human race will no longer be replacing itself by the early 2020s. Population growth after this will be mostly caused by people living longer, a factor that will diminish in significance from mid-century.

These shifts have important implications for global labour supply. China is ageing very rapidly, and its working-age population will begin to shrink within a few years. Relaxing the one-child policy might have some positive impact in the very long run, but China is already past the tipping point, pushed there by the combined effect of gender imbalance and a very skewed age structure.

The number of women of child-bearing age (15-49 years) in China will drop 8 per cent between 2010 and 2020, another 10 per cent in the 2020s and, if not corrected, at an even faster pace thereafter. Thus, China will have to withdraw an increasing proportion of its female workforce and deploy it for reproduction and childcare. Even if China can engineer this, it implies an immediate outflow from the workforce, with the benefits lagging by twenty-five years.

Meanwhile, the labour force has peaked or is close to

peaking in most major economies. Germany, Japan, and Russia already have declining workforces. The United States is one of a handful of advanced countries with a growing workforce, owing to its relative openness to immigration. But this may change as the source countries become richer and undergo rapid declines in birth rates. Thus, many developed countries will have to consider how to keep people working productively well into their Seventies.

India, the only large economy whose workforce will grow in sufficient scale over the next three decades, may partly balance the declines expected in other major economies. But, with birth rates declining there, too, current trends suggest that its population will probably stabilise at 1.55 billion in the early 2050s, a full decade ahead of—and 170 million people below—the UN's forecast.

Given this, it is likely that world population will peak at nine billion in the 2050s, a half-century sooner than generally anticipated, followed a sharp decline. One could argue that this is a good thing, in view of the planet's limited carrying capacity. But, when demographic dynamics turn, the world will have to confront a different set of problems.

(This piece was originally published in *Project Syndicate*, October 2011)

# INVESTMENT BINGE IN AMERICA WILL NOW DRIVE THE NEXT BOOM-BUST CYCLE

The IMF-World Bank meetings took place earlier this month in Washington DC. It is the annual jamboree for central bankers, finance ministry officials and senior economists from around the world.

As usual, the official statements paid homage to inclusive growth and the need for global coordination. However, a careful reading of discussions and statements suggests a subtle shift in how economists and policymakers hope to break out of the 'new mediocre' of tepid growth and deflation. In turn, this provides a clue to how the world economy may evolve over the next few years.

The IMF estimates that the world economy grew by 3.1 per cent in 2016 and that it will accelerate to 3.4 per cent next year. This is not an especially poor performance by historical standards. But there seems to be an almost unanimous view that the risks are all skewed to the downside. Many factors are cited: Brexit, China's internal adjustment away from investment-driven growth, the gridlocked European economy and so on. None of this is new.

What's more interesting is the growing tolerance of economists and policymakers for economic strategies that would have been condemned till a few years ago as unsustainable. The IMF's latest World Economic Outlook, for instance, gently suggests that governments should explore fiscal options 'even when fiscal space is limited'. The advice is couched in careful words, but the message is unmistakable.

This is interesting given that many governments, especially those of advanced countries, are already heavily indebted (even without counting pensions promised to a rapidly ageing population). Moreover, the IMF advises governments to pursue fiscal policies that 'support near-term growth and future productive capacity'. This is economist-speak aimed at encouraging public investment in infrastructure.

It is interesting that this is being recommended when the abysmal condition of physical infrastructure in the US has been brought up repeatedly in the presidential campaign. The Trump camp may have been more vocal about this, but several Clinton-leaning economists have also been arguing for greater investment in roads, bridges, airports and so on. The growing clamour for infrastructure investment in not surprising. Who would have thought at the turn of the century that Delhi and Mumbai would soon enjoy better airports than New York?

What is interesting is that politicians and economists seem to agree on this one thing. So, what are the implications of US infrastructure spending for the world economy?

The most obvious first-round impact of higher infrastructure spending will be stronger domestic demand. GDP growth has dropped to 1.6 per cent this year from 2.6 per cent in 2015, and one may feel that an investment splurge is just what is needed.

However, note that unemployment is down to 4.9 per cent from a peak of 9.6 per cent in 2010. The IMF similarly estimates that the country's output gap, which peaked at 4.7 per cent in 2009, has now effectively closed. In other words, the US will be attempting to accelerate an economy that is running close to full capacity. Matters would be exacerbated if tough immigration curbs are also introduced.

The second constraint is that a significant portion of the investment will have to be publicly sponsored even if the private sector is roped in. Government debt has gone up over the last fifteen years from 55 per cent of GDP to 108 per cent, and continues to creep up. A public investment binge will make the US even more indebted.

Third, the US savings rate is now back to the pre-crisis level of 18 per cent of GDP while investment rate is around 20 per cent. History suggests that the savings rate will not rise much further, so an increase in the investment rate would directly feed the country's current account deficit.

In other words, we would return to global imbalances with the US running a large deficit and China, which is allowing the renminbi (CNY, Chinese yuan) to drift weaker, running a large surplus.

Putting all this together, the next two years could see a debt-fuelled investment boom in the US, which generates domestic demand at a time that the economy is close to full employment. In turn, this would feed a trade deficit and inflation for non-tradables (although prices of tradables may still be held down by China).

## STOCK UP FOR THE DRY DAYS

The Fed may respond with higher rates but it will likely remain behind the curve. Meanwhile, the world would enjoy a period of better growth but return to large global imbalances too. Pessimists would argue that increased indebtedness and international imbalances would render such a cycle unsustainable. This is certainly true.

But the fact is that the world has never grown in a state of equilibrium. Every period of growth in history has been driven by large imbalances and distortions that ultimately undermined the phase. This time, the stresses in the system are already visible before the cycle takes off. Investors and businesses should strap in for the ride and remember to make provisions for the bust.

(This piece was originally published in *The Economic Times*, October 2016)

# IS BREXIT REALLY IRRATIONAL?

The results of the Brexit referendum have already crashed the world's financial markets and forced British Prime Minister David Cameron to resign.

So, was the vote for Brexit driven by irrational xenophobia? What are the long-term implications of Britain leaving the EU? What political lessons can the rest of the world learn?

It is very likely that the unwinding of Britain's relationship with Europe will involve some pain. The 'Remain' campaign hammered in this point. But, ironically, a majority of those who voted for 'Leave' would probably agree too. However, such historic events occur once in a generation and cannot be judged in terms of GDP growth rates for a couple of years.

Existing economic theory has little to say about the long-term impact of such structural shifts. This is why this mandate should be analysed through the lens of history, not economics. So, let it be clear that the voters were not being irrational by ignoring the economic pundits, as it is the wrong framework of reference.

One of the lessons of long-range history is that such shifts can trigger a spiral of events with major consequences. The decision to allow border crossings through the Berlin Wall in 1989, for instance, led to the collapse of the Soviet Union. The problem is that ex ante it is very difficult to predict the chain of events.

It is quite possible that after Brexit, the EU will reform itself and stage a comeback while Britain becomes a backwater struggling to hold on to Scotland. However, we could also see Europe get gridlocked by competing regional demands while Britain uses its new-found policy flexibility to rebuild itself.

A completely different set of outcomes is also possible. Given the radical uncertainties of long-range history, it is not irrational for people to want to take control of their destiny even if it increases short-term risk.

As an analogy, think of the British voter as the crew of a ship that is slowly drifting towards dangerous rocks. One option is to do nothing and hope the current will change and guide the ship away from danger. The other is to take control of the ship even if it means that one has to steer into a big storm.

Choosing the latter is not irrational. So, it is quite possible that history will judge Britain's decision kindly. After all, when Henry VIII opted for Brexit in the sixteenth century, the English were threatened with eternal damnation. As it turned out, it was the great Holy Roman empire that was wrecked by civil war and bankruptcy.

Even as we hold our judgement on the long-term

consequences of Brexit, there are some important political lessons that can be drawn.

As others have pointed out, the vote for Brexit is part of a revolt against a globalised elite that is concentrated in New York, London and the Silicon Valley, but also sprinkled across Singapore, Hong Kong, Dubai, Paris, south Mumbai and central Delhi.

It includes members of the political class, business, media, NGOs and elite academia. United by Ivy League and Oxbridge education, conferences in Switzerland and webs of influence, this elite justifies itself as working 'to make the world a better place'.

The non-elite have now begun to ask why those who claim to be giving away their money to improve the world need to protect their wealth in overseas tax havens or in charitable foundations. Surely, in an age of public indebtedness, the first step to improving the world is to pay one's fair share of taxes.

There is a suspicion that the money is used, instead, to buy influence through awards, financial grants, international conferences, buying media coverage and so on.

Justified or not, this rage against the global elite is a reality across the world and is partly responsible for the rise of Donald Trump in the US. A key mistake of Britain's 'Remain' campaign was to ask members of the same elite—from US President Barack Obama to celebrities from the entertainment industry—to campaign for them. Far from helping the cause, it entrenched suspicions that the international elite was pushing its own agenda.

This feeling was further inflamed when media pundits repeatedly stated that only the uneducated and the poor wanted to leave the EU, as if their lack of degrees made their opinions worthless.

The key lesson is that one cannot win over voters by patronisingly speaking down to them or implying that they are stupid or racist. Trump may be an unlikely and flawed leader of an anti-establishment movement but he has touched on underlying concerns that need to be taken seriously, not dismissed with disdain.

Meanwhile, the rise in uncertainty brings both risks and opportunities for India. On the one hand, export markets may be affected by a lack of confidence. On the other, commodity prices and global interest rates may remain low for an extended period. Indian policymakers should use the opportunity to cut interest rates and get the banking system going.

Brexit is neither good nor bad for India. It's mostly about how the country responds to the new situation.

(This piece was originally published in *The Economic Times*, June 2016)

# TRUMPONOMICS 101: DECODING DONALD TRUMP'S ECONOMIC VISION

Even as dust settles from the US elections, the world is wondering what President Donald Trump means for the world. Given that he said many unorthodox things on the campaign trail, there is a great deal of speculation about what he will do when actually deciding policy. He not only has a temperament and a mandate to break from the past, he has also been gifted a Republican-run Congress that will place fewer restraints on him.

There are many policy areas where we've little idea about Donald Trump's preferences. The campaign was so much about personalities that policies were barely discussed. Interestingly, we have greater clarity on his probable economic strategy. It is highly likely that the Trump administration will attempt the largest infrastructure buildout since Eisenhower. The intersection of several factors point to this.

First, candidate Trump repeatedly mentioned the appalling state of America's infrastructure in virtually all his speeches.

He is not the only person to have made this point. But it must be central to his thinking as he hammered at it over and over again.

Second, a big boost in infrastructure spending plays to both his strength as a builder as well as to his core constituency, the white working class. A rise in construction and roadworks is a direct transfer of jobs to this group.

Third, the consensus among technocrats has shifted significantly in favour of an investment-driven approach. As mentioned in an earlier piece, even IMF's conservative economists are advocating fiscal policies that 'support near-term growth and future productive capacity'.

So how will this investment boom be funded? Much of the spending will have to come from a government which is already under debt. Public debt has gone up in the last fifteen years from 55 per cent of the GDP to 108 per cent. So, the irony will be that a Republican-run Congress will be asked to run up even more debt.

Moreover, this investment-led strategy will be attempted at the time that unemployment is down at 4.9 per cent and the output gap (IMF estimates) has dropped from a peak of 4.7 per cent in 2009 to almost zero. This means that wages and prices of domestic non-tradables will begin to rise even as the current account deficit widens.

This brings us to the second irony of Trump's likely economic strategy: it will make US imports rise sharply. Restrictions and tariffs will change the mix of imported goods, but will not really change the quantum.

Thus, we are likely to be heading into a world where a

debt-driven investment boom in the US will revive world growth but also lead us back to large global imbalances. A steadily slowing Chinese economy, unable to sustain its own investment-led strategy, should be willing to fund the US deficit.

Critics will argue that this is an unsustainable economic model. But all periods of economic expansion in history have been underpinned by disequilibrium.

If Trump's investment strategy creates genuine productive assets, it is not obviously worse than Obama's social sector spending or the private consumption spending of the previous decade.

The demand dynamics and risks of this economic approach are relatively clear. Less obvious are the geopolitical implications of pursuing this strategy at a time when the rules of the international game are likely to change.

Since the Second World War, and even more so after the Soviet Union's collapse, the world order has been underpinned by a set of institutions, rules and unstated assumptions controlled by a class of technocrats, think tanks, academics, media pundits and lobbyists concentrated in Washington DC (and their friends in New York, London, etc).

It is they who decide the contours of the conversation on everything from climate change to West Asian strategy. The cozy power of this second-order elite is already being challenged by the rise of India and China, Brexit and so on. Trump, for his own political reasons, may radically reconfigure it.

What if Trump forces changes in global trade treaties?

What if he snubs Europeans who mocked him by backing a Russian, Brazilian or Indian to head the IMF? What if he disregards the large ecosystem of climate change experts and opts for a completely different approach? It is impossible to predict the impact of such shifts. But history shows that such changes often have unintended consequences.

The global consequences and risks of President Trump's likely economic strategy are, relatively speaking, predictable. The problem is that he may simultaneously attempt to change the underlying assumptions of the international order.

It is not possible ex ante to predict how this may change the way the world functions. For now, investors should buckle in for a faster-growing but imbalanced world.

(This piece was originally published in *The Economic Times*, November 2016)

# GO BEYOND STATISTICS

The world is reeling from two major crises, the financial/economic crisis and the crisis of climate change and ecological collapse. Both are a result of the same human error, a colossal misallocation of resources, financial capital in one case and natural capital on the other. A combination of counter-cyclical policies and time will eventually get us out of the financial mess. However, climate change and catastrophic environmental degradation threaten human civilisation as we know it.

Many blame globalisation and capitalism for the large-scale misallocation of resources. However, isolationism and socialism provide no alternative; we tried them for decades with disastrous results. A market-based system is clearly more efficient. The problem is not with the tools of capitalism but the failure to define its goals. The power of the markets is being harnessed to maximise the wrong paradigm.

The most commonly used paradigm for measuring human progress is provided by national income accounts and, more specifically, Gross Domestic Product (GDP). Virtually all economic policy-making is oriented directly or indirectly towards maximising GDP growth. It is so ubiquitous that people forget it is an entirely artificial construct created in the 1940s as part of the war effort.

Of course, rulers from ancient times have kept some record of economic activity for taxation purposes. National accounts as we know them were created during the Second World War by Richard Stone and James Meade, with support from John Maynard Keynes, as a way to keep track of war-time economic activity. Given the circumstances, their framework was necessarily 'industrial' in its essence, without space for niceties like environmental degradation and socio-demographic developments.

Post-war, this framework was adapted to create the GDP number now used. Unfortunately, the system remains an arbitrary way to measure value creation, especially in areas relating to externalities, social and natural capital. For instance, if we cut down a pristine rain forest, we are destroying value in terms of biodiversity, watersheds, carbon sequestration, flood control, non-timber forest produce and so on. Yet, in the current system, destruction of value will show up as GDP growth from logging!

This does not mean the creators of GDP were unaware of its limitations. In his Nobel Memorial Lecture in 1984, Richard Stone stated, 'The three pillars on which analysis of society ought to rest are studies of economic, socio-demographic and environmental phenomena.' He added that his work had focused mostly on economic accounting and he had not spent much time on environmental accounting even though 'environmental issues, such as pollution, land use and non-renewable resources offer plenty of scope for accounting.' In short, the creators of GDP thought of it as work-in-progress. Unfortunately, the world has continued to focus much of its energy on maximising an incomplete and out-of-date paradigm.

There are ways to adjust for the shortcomings of GDP. One is to create additional matrices for measuring progress. The Human Development Index and Carbon Footprint are concepts that can be used to enhance the raw GDP approach. Unfortunately, they have failed to gain a serious following beyond the world of activists and conferences because these measures lack the simplicity of a single GDP number.

The only real alternative then is to recalibrate GDP itself to reflect genuine value generation. This can be done by assigning monetary values to things like water pollution, deforestation, land degradation and other changes in the stock of natural capital. Similar adjustments can be made to account for changes in human capital stock (health, education etc.). The result would be a new GDP number more closely reflecting true value generated by various human activities.

This approach has many advantages. First, GDP is understood by policy-makers and the general public. It's a single number simple to grasp and apply. The new GDP number would merely replace the current measure. Once national income incorporates these changes, the 'development' versus 'environment' debate will narrow.

Second, we have a whole range of tools and methodologies

to value natural/human capital. These had not been developed when GDP was originally conceived. Incorporating new techniques will allow us to seamlessly adjust to existing national accounts. Studies by the Green Accounting for Indian States Project have already demonstrated that it is possible to make these adjustments even for a large, complex developing country like India. The data can be calculated by sector and state. The results are astounding. For instance, water quality in Uttar Pradesh's rivers is now so bad, it would alone take off 17.5 per cent from the state's GDP!

Third, all policy-making is about trade-offs. Often these are difficult trade-offs that compare apples with oranges: the benefits of building a dam versus those of retaining an existing forest or settlement. By assigning monetary values to creation/depletion of natural and human capital, the new GDP framework can effectively 'internalise' various externalities. For instance, it allows us to work out who compensates whom and by how much. In turn, this will allow for far more informed public debate.

GDP is not a god-given measure of development. As I have said before, the existing model of national accounts was a fallout of the Second World War. There is every reason we should update it. When we say that GDP grew by eight per cent, we should really mean that we added eight per cent more value.

(This piece was originally published in *The Times of India*, February 2009)

# WILL US FEDERAL RESERVE'S RATE HIKE MAKE GLOBAL CAPITAL EXPENSIVE?

As widely expected, the US Federal Reserve decided to hike its benchmark rates by twenty-five basis points. The statement also suggested that future hikes will be gradual. A small hike, combined with a dovish statement, is not unreasonable for an economy where the unemployment rate has fallen to 5 per cent. Yet, several commentators seem concerned that this could make capital too expensive for the global economy, especially struggling emerging markets.

The question is—will even small interest rate hikes by the US Fed make global capital expensive over the next year? In order to answer this question, one must first recognise that the real source of cheap capital (and deflation) in the world is not the United States, but China. The Asian giant singlehandedly accounts for more than a quarter of all the world's investment and savings. Its dominance is driven by the fact that it saves and invests almost half of its eleven trillion economy. The problem is that such an investment effort cannot be sustained in an economy that has brand new infrastructure and suffers excess capacity in almost every sector. Moreover, its workforce is now shrinking and the new services sectors simply need less capital.

The dynamic is already visible: China's domestic investment rate declined from 47 per cent of GDP in 2011 to 44.3 per cent in 2015 ( IMF estimate). Given the experience of former investment-driven economies like Japan, it is reasonable to expect this rate to drop to somewhere in 35 per cent range over the next decade. However, the experience of rapidly ageing societies also shows that the savings rate will not decline quite so quickly. We have already seen this in China with the savings rate falling only from 48.8 per cent to 47.4 per cent between 2011 and 2015. In other words, rising consumption will not fully compensate slowing investment.

For China's domestic economy, this means that GDP growth rate will steadily drift down even if the authorities manage to smoothen the transition. The important implication from a global perspective is that the persistent gap between China's savings and investment rates will generate excess savings that will show up as large current account surpluses. Indeed, the surplus has already jumped from 136 billion in 2011 to an estimated 348 billion in 2015. In turn, this surplus will flood the world as capital outflows (i.e., Chinese investments in other countries). This could happen through direct investments or indirectly through institutions like the Brics Bank and Asian Infrastructure Investment Bank.

The pipeline of cheap capital from China is potentially so large and persistent that it could hold down the cost of long-term global capital even if the US Fed keeps tightening. As the world economy is a closed system, someone will have to run a deficit in order to absorb the excess savings being generated by China. The emerging economies just do not have the scale necessary to absorb such large sums. Europe has the scale, but does not seem to be in a position to ramp up spending. The best we can expect is that it does not add to the problem by generating its own surpluses. This brings us back to the US. It is still the world's largest economy and its investment rate has barely climbed back 20 per cent of GDP this year. Therefore, theoretically it could ramp up its investment effort and absorb the excess capital (a consumption binge would also achieve this although one hopes that lessons have been learned from the pre-2007 period).

Infrastructure is the most obvious sector that could absorb large amounts of capital. The US now has arguably the worst infrastructure of any major developed country; some of it is poor even by emerging market standards. The problem is that most infrastructure ultimately needs government spending and the US government is not likely to go on an investment spree. Gross government debt now stands at 104 per cent of GDP and is refusing to decline despite the revival in growth. Political hurdles will also hold down infrastructure spending in 2016. Higher rates will certainly not help the case.

In other words, the cost of long-term global capital will only rise if the US absorbs most of the excess savings emanating from China.

Unfortunately, short of yet another debt-fuelled consumption binge, the US looks unlikely to absorb enough capital. If the Fed keeps hiking rates under these circumstances, we will have a stronger dollar, but not necessarily higher long-term rates for the rest of the world.

In fact, it could potentially cause deflation that would allow countries like India to reduce interest rates further. If as a result the rupee keeps declining along with other currencies against the dollar, so be it. Even China is increasingly managing its exchange rate against a basket.

To summarise: the world economy will only generate growth by reverting to large global imbalances. In such a situation, the US will be again sucking in a large quantum of imports from the rest of the world. The alternative is that the world economy continues to drift in limbo due to the US economy's unwillingness to run the necessary deficits. However, global capital will remain cheap in this circumstance. Both outcomes offer opportunities for India.

(This piece was originally published in *The Economic Times*, December 2015)

# THE LEFT PARALYSIS

When the then Prime Minister P.V. Narasimha Rao and Finance Minister Manmohan Singh initiated the reform process in 1991, I was an undergraduate in Delhi University. Some reforms did get done in subsequent years, but sadly the bulk still remains to be done after quarter of a century. Indeed, we are still debating many of the issues that I remember discussing in the college canteen: privatisation, enforcement of contracts, administrative reforms, simplification of the tax system and so on.

There may be many factors that explain why India has been such a reluctant reformer—bureaucratic obstructionism, political populism, fiscal constraints, the small pool of technocratic talent and so on. However, a major reason is that the intellectual case for reforms was never really made. Recall that it was not a change of mindset, but a serious economic crisis that forced the government to start liberalising the economy in 1991.

In other words, India's intellectual establishment remained, and still largely remains, wedded to the idea that Nehru's socialist economic model was essentially good; if only it had been implemented properly. Even when it became quite apparent by the 1970s that the model was a failure, establishment economist Raj Krishna coined the term 'Hindu rate of growth' to describe lacklustre economic performance. The term slyly rebranded the failures of socialism as those of India's social structures and dominant religion.

The message was that India had failed the Nehruvian vision and not the other way around. That is why Manmohan Singh, even while announcing reforms in his budget speech of 29 February 1992, felt it necessary to start by saying, 'Our nation will remain eternally grateful to Jawaharlal Nehru for his vision....'

So, why was the Nehruvian worldview so dominant? Part of the explanation is that it gelled with the prevailing intellectual milieu of the time that saw the Soviet Union as a genuine alternative. However, India's first prime minister also benefited from the fact that all other leaders who could have provided different visions died soon after Independence: Mahatma Gandhi, Sardar Vallabhbhai Patel, Syama Prasad Mookerjee and B.R. Ambedkar (controversy still rages on what happened to another alternative, Subhas Bose).

The only survivor was C. Rajagopalachari, who bitterly opposed Nehru's socialism and prophetically warned of 'Licence Raj'. After being systematically sidelined in the Congress party, Rajaji would set up the Swatantra Party in 1959 to vociferously oppose the socialist economic model.

# THE DOLLAR'S LONG TAIL

e ongoing economic crisis and the persistent deficits
ced by the United States have increasingly called into
n the dollar's role as the world's anchor currency.
noves to internationalise China's renminbi have led
pation of a looming shift in the global monetary
any prominent economists, including members of a
ions panel headed by the Nobel laureate economist
litz, are recommending a Global Reserve System
he dollar's hegemony. But the long history of
r currencies suggests that the dollar's days on
r from over.

times, India ran a large trade surplus with
pire. As Pliny wrote in the first century,
d in which India did not take fifty million
om Rome. That trade imbalance implied a
on gold and silver coins, causing shortages
Rome. In modern terms, the Romans faced

By now, he was in his Eighties and the party would fizzle out after some initial success.

Perhaps one can forgive Nehru and his generation for having been swayed by the intellectual fads of their times. What is far more puzzling is the persistence of the socialist-era mindset in the intellectual establishment, despite its glaring failures and the obvious gains from the sporadic episodes of reforms. We saw some reforms during 1991–93, followed by faster GDP growth in subsequent years. But the reforms themselves petered out once the crisis was over.

There was another period of reforms during 2000–2003 under the Vajpayee regime. This too led to better economic performance, but again was not followed up with new reforms in subsequent years. Instead, we saw regressive measures such as the Right to Education (RTE) Act which was deliberately meant to undermine any private sector response to the failures of the State-run school system (but contains nothing to actually improve government schools).

So, the question is why RTE can be pushed through, but not GST? After all, there was no large-scale popular movement demanding RTE in any part of the country. The answer lies in the near total dominance of all intellectual institutions by the Left. For every reform-minded Raghuram Rajan, there were platoons of the National Advisory Council. Even after Prime Minister Narendra Modi came to power with a clear reformist manifesto in 2014, almost all intellectual institutions—think tanks, universities, the media—remain overwhelmingly Left-dominated.

Its dominance over the intellectual establishment has its

roots in the systematic 'ethnic cleansing' of all non-Left thinkers since the 1950s. One of its early victims was liberal economist, B.R. Shenoy who questioned Nehru's economics. He was squeezed out of the establishment and persecuted, but continued to write—against socialist planning.

In 1975, he wrote, 'We adopted these policies as a means to an end, not as a political way of life, as in communist countries. It is time that we replaced them by policies that have stood the test of logic and empirical evidence.' He went on to argue that socialist economics was at the root of all-pervasive corruption. It is telling that these critiques have been erased from public memory, but Raj Krishna's disingenuous 'Hindu rate of growth' is still widely used.

The result of the systematic cleansing was that there were no non-Left academics in the social sciences field in India by the early 1990s. This is the reason that even as the Soviet Union was collapsing and India was being forced to liberalise, my lecturers in Delhi University were still waxing eloquent about the benefits of the P.C. Mahalanobis model and arcane intricacies of Yevgeni Preobrazhensky's 'primitive accumulation' theory.

Since the 1990s, the more explicitly Soviet-derived material has been removed from curriculums, but they remain heavily dominated by the Left. Thus, economics students are mostly taught material written by Amartya Sen and his stable of academics, but exposed only in passing to the thoughts of Friedrich Hayek, Milton Friedman or Jagdish Bhagwati, Sen's intellectual rival. Even when non-Left thinkers are included, their ideas are lumped together

as exotic curiosities to be critiqued, rather than imb' Shenoy is still deemed too dangerous to be taught v The situation is much worse in other discipli sociology and history.

The result is that even those advocating cha using language and frameworks derived from t' with roots going back all the way to Nehru This is very damaging to the cause of refo starting point of each debate is heavily s struggle to push through even the simr is why there needs to be a wider r bringing greater plurality of though establishment.

Note that I am not advocatir dominance of the Left should dominance of the Right. Howe that some sort of balance moreover, that debates pla than on ideologies and p making shift from argu the argumentative In' things done.

(This piece was orig' 2016)

Rome responded by reducing the gold/silver content (the ancient equivalent of monetisation), which led to sustained inflation in the empire. But the frequent discovery of debased Roman coins in India suggests that they continued to be accepted internationally long after it must have been obvious that its gold or silver content had fallen.

In the sixteenth century, Spain emerged as a superpower following its conquest of South America. Between 1501 and 1600, seventeen million kilograms of pure silver and 181,000 kilograms of pure gold flowed from the Americas to Spain, which spent the money on wars in the Netherlands and elsewhere. This increase in liquidity caused both an economic boom and inflation across Europe.

Despite this wealth, Spain became increasingly indebted, eventually defaulting three times—in 1607, 1627, and 1649—and heading into sharp geopolitical decline. Yet Spanish silver coins (known as pieces of eight or Spanish dollars) remained the main currency used in world trade right up to the American Revolutionary War. In fact, the Spanish coin remained legal tender in the US until 1857—long after Spain itself had ceased to be a major power.

By the middle of the nineteenth century, the world was functioning on a bi-metal system based on gold and silver. But, following the British example, most major countries had shifted to a gold standard by the 1870s.

The Bank of England stood ready to convert a pound sterling into an ounce of (11/122 fine) gold on demand. That system was disrupted by the First World War, but Britain went back to a gold peg in 1925. However, as the Great

Depression took root, the Bank of England was forced to choose between providing liquidity to banks and honouring the gold peg. It opted for the former in 1931.

Yet pound sterling continued to be a major world currency until well after the Second World War. Even as late as 1950—more than a half-century after the US had replaced Britain as the world's largest industrial power—55 per cent of foreign exchange reserves were held in sterling, and many countries continued to peg their currencies to it.

Three things should be clear from this history. First, a global monetary system based on precious metals does not resolve the fundamental imbalances of a global economic system. Second, precious metals do not resolve the problem of inflation. And, finally, the anchor currency and the underlying eco-system of world trade often outlive the geopolitical decline of the anchor country by decades.

A new economic order was established after the Second World War with the US as the anchor country. The Bretton Woods system linked the US dollar to gold at thirty-five dollars per ounce, with other currencies linked to the dollar (though occasionally allowed to make adjustments).

The flaw in the system was that it underpinned global economic expansion for only as long as the US was willing to provide dollars by running up deficits—the same deficits that would eventually undermine America's ability to maintain the thirty-five dollars/ounce gold price. In 1961, the US responded by creating the London Gold Pool, which obliged other countries to reimburse the US for half of its gold losses. But this arrangement quickly bred discontent, with France leaving the Gold Pool in 1967. The Bretton Woods system collapsed four years later.

Or did it? Despite the problems of the 1970s, the dollar remained the world's dominant currency, with successive generations of Asian countries pegging their exchange rates to it. As with the Bretton Woods system, a peripheral economy (for example, China) could grow very rapidly even as the anchor economy (the US) enjoyed cheap financing. China's relative rise did not diminish the dollar's role—and may even have enhanced it. Indeed, like the Japanese during their period of rapid growth, the Chinese have, until recently, resisted internationalisation of the renminbi.

So, are we entering a post-dollar world? Despite all the pain caused by the Great Recession, there is no sign that the world is forsaking the greenback. Investors remain willing to finance the US at rock-bottom interest rates, and the nominal trade-weighted index of the dollar has not collapsed. Even if China replaces the US as the world's largest economy in a bit over a decade (no sure thing), an anchor currency can be more resilient than the economic and geopolitical dominance of its country of origin. That is why the dollar will most likely remain the dominant global currency long after the US has been surpassed.

(This piece was originally published in *Project Syndicate*, November 2011)

# THE CUSTOMISATION REVOLUTION

The last two decades were the era of hypermarkets—massive superstores that could dazzle customers with an astonishing array of standardised products. But there are signs that the superstore's age of dominance may be over. In recent months, hypermarkets around the world—Walmart, Tesco, Carrefour—have announced results that fell short of expectations. Conventional wisdom is that this reflects the economic cycle, but it may be the first sign of a more fundamental shift.

The world's economic history can be seen as a race between transportation and communications. Transportation innovations allow supply chains to carry increasingly large quantities, which thereby encourages standardisation. Communications innovations, on the other hand, allow for better specification of design, quality, quantity, and time of delivery, which tends to encourage customisation. The dominant economic model of any era emerges from the relative evolution of these two technologies.

288

In ancient times, transportation technology was poor, and the production of most goods was local. Since consumers and producers could communicate directly with each other, artisan manufacturing was mostly customised. This was the age of the village blacksmith, weaver, potter, and cobbler.

\* \* \*

In the eighteenth century, shipping technology had improved to a considerable extent to allow for the creation of global supply chains. Cotton was one of the first industries to witness this shift. Slaves from Africa were used to growing cotton in southern United States, which was then shipped to English mills. The finished cloth was then exported to the rest of the world. The impact of this change on India's artisan weavers and spinners was profound. It is no coincidence that Mahatma Gandhi used the hand-turned spinning wheel as his symbol of protest against colonial rule.

By the early twentieth century, transportation technology witnessed major breakthroughs, including railways, the Suez Canal, the Panama Canal, automobiles, and even early airplanes. Ocean freight rates, for example, fell by 70 per cent between 1840 and 1910. But, while improvements in transportation also improved communications—steamships and railways could also carry letters—there were few *independent* innovations in communications, the main exception being the telegraph.

Good transportation with relatively underdeveloped communications meant that production was centralised at major transportation hubs, and production lines resembling those pioneered by the American automobile manufacturer Henry Ford were used to mass manufacture goods. Vertically integrated industrial structures were needed to minimise communication gaps between various stages of production. As mass manufacturing grew to dominate production, it was no longer possible for individual customers to specify requirements.

Ford famously summarised this shift: 'Any customer can have a car painted in any color that he wants,' he declared, 'so long as it is black.' Retailing migrated towards large department stores that could use vast selections of standardised products to substitute for customisation.

Then, in the 1950s, two further innovations—telephones and containerisation—brought another round of change. The telephone had been invented in the previous century, but it was only after the Second World War that the price of an international call fell to a level that was affordable for common business use. Meanwhile, containerisation dramatically improved the speed, reliability, and cost of transporting goods. By the 1970s, the Japanese had combined the two technologies to modularise production and create 'just-in-time' supply chains.

The communications revolution of the 1990s made supply chains even more efficient. One outcome was that hypermarkets could leverage scale, logistics, and lean inventories to squeeze prices and provide customers with unprecedented choice. Customer needs were met by providing a wide variety of standardised products—not through customisation.

One consequence of the democratisation of communications

technology is that it is now possible for customers to specify their requirements rather than hope that the available standardised products will suffice. The online retailer Amazon, for example, changed the bookstore game completely by offering almost infinite choice and large discounts. Nonetheless, first generation e-commerce still felt like a large hypermarket. At that point, it was not yet exploiting the new technology's ability to provide low-cost customisation.

Today, near-customisation is rapidly becoming the norm. Electronic tablets and mobile devices, for instance, allow us to access increasingly specialised applications. Similarly, YouTube has just invested hundred million dollars to create dozens of television-like channels that will cater to audiences with narrowly defined interests. Even Amazon is gradually transforming itself from an internet hypermarket to something closer to a clearing house that matches customer requests with near customised products.

So, will hypermarkets suffer the same fate as bookstores? Some, already aware of the new reality, are investing heavily in new systems. But, even if the companies survive, the old business model probably will not. Companies and customers should prepare themselves for a new era of mass customisation.

(This piece was originally published in *Project Syndicate*, March 2012)

# RISE OF TOMORROW'S MIDDLE CLASS

At the heart of India's economic and cultural resurgence over the last two decades is an urban middle class that has had the confidence to take on the world. This is not unique to India—from nineteenth century Britain to modern China, the self-reinforcing expansion of the middle class has been a key driver of growth. India has barely embarked on this journey. However, the future is not an extrapolation of today's urban middle class but the creation of a brand new social group with its own attitudes, affiliations and dynamics. Think about the shop assistant at the new mall, the call centre worker pestering you with phone calls about various insurance schemes, or even the newly minted sports hero standing on the medals podium at the recent Commonwealth Games. These are not the children of yesterday's middle class. Understanding this new group is key to understanding India's future.

# A HISTORY OF THE MIDDLE CLASS

A proto-middle class existed in India prior to the British period, consisting of petty Mughal officials, shopkeepers, master craftsmen, priests and scribes. However, they were not a middle class in the modern sense. They would not quite have imbibed the very middle-class value that one can use education and hard work to better one's position. There is a difference between respect for learning and seeing it as an agent for change. From the middle of the nineteenth century, the mindset began to shift as the ideas of the Industrial Revolution began to seep into the major cities of British India. Social values were transformed by the efforts of reformers like Ram Mohan Roy and Ishwar Chandra Vidyasagar. At the same time, the growing use of the English language provided access to technological, political and cultural innovations of the West. Thus, the Indian middle class was born. By the early twentieth century, it was influential enough to provide many of the key leaders of India's freedom movement.

With Independence, the upper echelons of the existing middle class became the new elite. Others gained from the expansion of public sector jobs in the Fifties and early Sixties. Some new blood may have been sucked in, but much of this growth was from the demographic growth of the existing middle class. Remember that job aspirants of the Fifties would have been born in the Thirties when middle-class women commonly had three or more children. In other words, the public sector did not cause much vertical social mobility. Its main impact was horizontal by re-allocating its employees to jobs that were away from their home provinces. Housing colonies had to be built to house IIT professors, engineers working for SAIL and so on. The private sector also mimicked this general trend. In turn, it created a whole generation of middle-class children who grew up together in housing colonies and with a shared experience—Chitrahaar on Doordarshan; the Fiat or scooter that was replaced by the Maruti 800; and the unending sequence of exams. From the early Nineties, they began to inter-marry. For the first time, there was a truly pan-Indian middle class. Till now, the Indian middle class had been the sum of the Tamil middle class, Bengali middle class, Punjabi middle class and so on. However, by the Nineties, we had a social group whose members had more in common with each other than with those of their caste or province of origin.

When India liberalised its economy in the Nineties, it was this group that benefited the most from the boom in white-collar jobs. Some of the members of the group even set up businesses and prospered. Still, the middle class continued to be dominated by those whose parents and grandparents would have been recognisably middle class. This is now changing.

## YESTERDAY'S MIDDLE CLASS

The Indian middle class is much smaller than casual media reports suggest. My calculations suggest that, adjusted for purchasing power, this group is currently around 60-70 million by most international standards (far less than the

300 million that is quoted in corporate boardrooms). It is reasonable to expect, however, that it will grow very fast with the current trajectory of economic growth—perhaps by four times in the next twenty years. But, where will they all come from?

Note that the existing middle class will not provide this expanded group with an anchor population. Their numbers are being depleted by prosperity (many have graduated to being upper class) and emigration (which middle-class family doesn't have someone abroad)? Even more importantly, there has been a very sharp decline in birth rates. By the Eighties, the average middle-class family had two kids. My guesstimate is that, today the average middle-class woman produces around 1.2 children. This is half the level needed to keep a population stable. In other words, when the Indian middle class hits 250-300 million in 2030, barely a tenth of it will be drawn from the pre-existing pool. What does this mean?

## IMPLICATIONS

The first implication is that we are entering an era of unprecedented upward mobility. We can see this in all arenas. For instance, it was common for officers in the armed forces to be drawn from distinguished families, often with a military past. Now we are witnessing large-scale intake from more modest backgrounds. The same can be said of the civil service. Similarly, the average entrant to an IIT is no longer from institutions like St Xavier's and St Columba's only, but more likely from a coaching centre in Kota.

Second, we need to recognise that this process will be linked strongly to the wider process of urbanisation. The parents of tomorrow's middle class work in our cities today as chauffeurs, janitors and shop assistants. Like the parents of several medal-winners at the Delhi Commonwealth Games, they are systematically investing in their children's future. This is why they endure the indignity of a life in the slums, and in the long run, this shall have important implications for our urban policy. We need to change the way we think of slums, small towns and public housing—this is where the new middle class is being created.

Third, the new entrants are bound to bring different cultural attitudes with them. This has pros and cons. What may appear energetic in some situations, may appear brash in others. Most importantly, from a political perspective, this group will not have the old links of patronage that connected the elite with the old middle-class. The recent Adarsh real estate scam in Mumbai is a graphic example of this incestuous relationship. It is possible that the new entrants begin to ask uncomfortable questions about corruption and nepotism. Alternatively, it could take an approach that pays scant regard to the rules, further eroding the institutions of governance. Whatever it is, we can no longer ignore the new middle-India.

(This piece was originally published in *Business Standard*, November 2010)

# BRETTON WOODS III

Many analysts and observers believe that the global imbalances that characterised the world economy in the years before the 2008 crisis have substantially dissipated. But, while it is true that China's current-account surpluses and America's deficits have somewhat moderated since then, have the imbalances really been corrected? More important, can the post-crisis global economy enjoy both growth and balance?

To answer these questions, it is important to understand the imbalances' underlying dynamics. An economy's current account is the difference between its investment rate and its savings rate. In 2007, the United States had a savings rate of 14.6 per cent of GDP, but an investment rate of 19.6 per cent, generating a current-account deficit. By contrast, China had a fixed investment rate of 41.7 per cent of GDP and a savings rate of 51.9 per cent, reflected in a large surplus.

Since 2007, the US current-account deficit has narrowed, but not because of a higher savings rate. Rather, the external deficit has been squeezed by a collapse in investment activity, while America's overall savings rate has fallen below 13 per cent of GDP, owing to worsening government finances. Meanwhile, China's savings rate remains stubbornly high. The surplus has narrowed because investment has been ramped up even higher, to roughly 49 per cent of GDP. In other words, the Americans save even less today than they did before the crisis erupted, and the Chinese invest even more.

Any future recovery in the US economy will almost certainly trigger a revival in investment activity. American businesses have postponed much-needed capital spending and, with American airports and bridges in appalling condition by developed country standards, investment in infrastructure is crucial as well. Indeed, it is very likely that reviving growth will lead to larger current-account deficits, even if the savings rate improves and domestic energy production curtails oil and gas imports.

China has the opposite problem. In order to sustain growth, it needs to continue to invest half of its nine dollar trillion annual GDP—no easy task for a country that already has brand new highways and airports. In fact, over the next decade, as China attempts to move up the value chain into services and adjusts to a shrinking workforce, its investment requirements shrink, and its investment rate will fall sharply.

Of course, China's savings rate will also decline, but Japan's experience since the 1980s demonstrates how a sharp fall in investment can generate large and persistent current-account surpluses, even when the savings rate is falling and the currency is appreciating. Indeed, a stronger currency can paradoxically feed external surpluses, while discouraging investment in export-oriented industries.

The implication is that the post-crisis global economy will not be characterised by balance, but by a return to large macroeconomic imbalances. But, although many economists will consider this problematic, history shows that symbiotic imbalances have characterised virtually all periods of global economic expansion.

The Roman empire ran a persistent trade deficit with India for centuries. Although the resulting outflow of gold caused monetary debasement in the Roman empire, Indo-Roman trade remained the backbone of the global economy.

Similarly, Spain ran persistent deficits in the sixteenth and seventeenth centuries, paid for by Andean silver. The resulting flood of liquidity caused a global boom that benefited economies from Elizabethan England to Mughal India. Yet another period of rapid growth and globalisation was 1870-1913, which too wasn't characterised by balance; it was funded by the United Kingdom, acting as the world's 'bank'.

In the last sixty years, the US has underpinned global growth by running persistent current-account deficits. Under the Bretton Woods system, the US ran deficits that enabled war-torn Europe and Japan to rebuild. In return, Europe funded the US deficits.

The system broke down when European countries, particularly France, decided to stop funding those deficits. But the economic model persisted, with Asian economies stepping in to finance the US deficits, while using the country's market to grow rapidly. China is the latest and largest beneficiary of the economic model dubbed 'Bretton Woods II'. Clearly, periods of global growth are almost always characterised by symbiotic imbalances. But, while each of these episodes was characterised by macroeconomic distortions caused by the imbalances, they lasted for years, or even decades. So, the real question is what the next generation of symbiotic imbalances will look like.

It is likely that China will soon return to running very large current-account surpluses—potentially large enough to fund the US, with plenty left over for the rest of the world. As this capital cascades through the global financial system, it will re-inflate the economy.

In the 'Bretton Woods III' system, China will transform from 'factory to the world' to 'investor to the world'. Like all imbalanced systems, it will have its distortions, but the arrangement could last for many years.

(This piece was originally published in *Project Syndicate*, February 2013)

# IN PRAISE OF GLOBAL IMBALANCES

In recent weeks, there has been a chorus of opinion arguing for a sharp increase in global investment, particularly in infrastructure. Former US Treasury Secretary, Lawrence Summers asserted that public investment really is a free lunch, while IMF Managing Director, Christine Lagarde has argued that an investment boost is needed if the world economy is to 'overcome a new mediocre.'

These comments suggest that the world has been under-investing for many years. In fact, according to International Monetary Fund data, the current overall global investment rate, at 24.5 per cent of world GDP, is near the top of its long-term range. The issue is not a lack of overall investment, but the fact that a disproportionate share of it comes from China.

China's share of world investment has soared from 4.3 per cent in 1995 to an estimated 25.8 per cent this year. By contrast, the United States' share, which peaked at 36 per cent in 1985, has fallen to less than 18 per cent. The decline in Japan's share has been more dramatic, from a peak of 22 per cent in 1993 to just 5.7 per cent in 2013.

China dominates global investment because it saves and invests nearly half of its 10.5 dollar trillion economy. But this investment rate is likely to decline sharply over the next decade, because the country already boasts of new infrastructure, has excess manufacturing capacity in many sectors, and is trying to shift economic activity to services—which require less investment. Moreover, China's rapidly ageing population and declining working-age population will reduce long-term investment demand.

Because the current-account balance is the difference between the investment and savings rates, the decline in investment will generate large surpluses unless savings also decline. And the experience of other ageing societies, such as Germany and Japan, suggests that domestic investment falls faster than savings rates.

Thus, China can expect large external surpluses to transform the country from the world's workshop into its main financier. Indeed, the scale of capital outflows could be so large that long-term capital will remain cheap even after the world's major central banks tighten monetary policy. How the world absorbs those surpluses will define the next period of global economic expansion.

Emerging markets may be able to take some advantage of this low-cost financing. India would undoubtedly benefit, though it is unlikely to absorb a significant portion of China's excess savings. India's share of world investment is only 3.4 per cent; and even a large expansion will not compensate for a small decline in Chinese investment. Furthermore, East Asia's growth model has been sustained ultimately by mobilising rising domestic savings and pumping out exports. So, although India might initially absorb some international capital, it might ultimately prefer to build foreign reserves by running small external deficits or even a surplus.

Other emerging countries are also unlikely to absorb much of China's capital. Notwithstanding its advocacy of public investment spending, even the IMF accepts that a sudden increase in public investment is more likely to cause developing-country indebtedness than growth.

That is why calls by the IMF and others to scale up public infrastructure spending are really aimed at developed countries. Yet this, too, may prove insufficient. Germany's investment-savings gap is so large that, even if it increases domestic investment, the most we can expect from Europe is that it does not add to the global savings glut.

Only a revival in US infrastructure investment can create a sustained global economic recovery. The US has the necessary scale to absorb China's surplus, and its inadequate infrastructure provides plenty of avenues for fruitful investment.

Ironically, the IMF's new investment mantra ultimately leads back to large global imbalances. But, far from decrying this as a major failure of global policy coordination, economists should accept imbalances as the natural state of the world and try to manage the resulting distortions.

Indeed, almost every period of globalisation and prosperity has been accompanied by symbiotic imbalances. They have always caused economic distortions and political complaints, but many have endured for surprisingly long periods.

Consider, for example, how Indo-Roman trade drove the world economy in the first and second centuries AD. India ran a current-account surplus for centuries, while the Romans complained about the loss of gold, yet the system endured. Similarly, the first Bretton Woods system was sustained with European capital, and Bretton Woods II was fuelled by Asian capital, with the US providing the deficits in both cases. In other words, imbalanced systems can be surprisingly resilient.

There is no reason why Bretton Woods III would not experience similar imbalances. But if, for whatever reason, the global economy fails to take off, we will have to reconcile ourselves to a long period of mediocre growth in which cheap capital depresses yields, drives up asset prices, inflates bubbles, and seeks out trophy assets. These are not the sort of imbalances to which the world's policymakers should aspire.

(This piece was originally published in *Project Syndicate*, November 2014)

# WHY WE NEED A 'TRANSPARENCY OF RULES' ACT

The essential premise of all systems of governance is that common citizens follow the rules of the land. However, almost all discussion on governance focuses on only one side of the equation—on how the State should use the stick (and occasionally a carrot) to ensure that laws are followed. Note that there is a presumption here that all citizens know and understand what is required of them and, therefore, any deviation is either due to wilful defiance or lazy negligence. This is why ignorance of the law is not allowed as a defence in any court. In turn, this assumes that the citizen knows the rules or can easily find them. Unfortunately, this is no simple task in India.

We are all expected to navigate through a plethora of rules, procedures and forms that apply to routine activities like getting a driving licence, applying for a gas connection, setting up a business, building a house and so on. I am not talking here about the great laws that are contained in the Constitution or debated in parliament. I am referring to the little administrative rules and regulations that govern our daily lives. These rules are usually set by government departments, local bodies and other agencies. Even if the original guidelines are clear, these rules are inevitably subject to change. Very soon we find ourselves in a quagmire of modified sub-clauses, exemptions, internal contradictions and complex procedures.

Note that I am not commenting on the quality of the laws—that is a major issue in its own right. I am merely pointing out that it is nearly impossible for even the most law-abiding citizen to known exactly what to do. Thus, we routinely find ourselves at the mercy of petty officials and touts. Indeed, it sometimes feels that the whole framework has been deliberately set up for rent-seeking.

## FRAMEWORK FOR REFORM

Given the above situation, we need a fundamental change in the way common citizens are informed about the laws, rules and regulations that they are expected to follow. Here are three simple steps that would radically change the situation:

> First, it must be made mandatory that all rules, procedures and forms must be placed on the website of the relevant agency or department as well as prominently pasted on the office notice-board in English and Hindi (and/or local language). Today, we have an arbitrary system where some agencies put up

their rules on the web and some do not. More often than not, the information is partial, out-of-date or simply misleading. Under the new framework, a rule or procedure will be deemed not to apply unless the citizens have been given a fighting chance to know about it. If the rule on the website or notice-board is wrong or incomplete, then that is what applies. If a form is not mentioned clearly or provided, then it need not be filled out. This is not entirely a new principle because major laws, such as those passed by parliament, come into effect only after they have been notified in the Gazette of India. I am merely extending this to apply to all government rules and procedures.

Second, all laws, regulations and procedures must be presented as a coherent whole rather than as a series of circulars and notifications. At present, a citizen needs to follow a complex paper trail in order to understand what is expected of him/her. Even officials do not often know the current state of the law (or pretend not to know). I can understand that in the old days it may have been simpler to update rules by appending a sub-clause. This makes no sense today when it is easier to make the change in the main text and then highlight it using italics. Wikipedia provides a good illustration of how we can constantly update a certain text while allowing easy comparison with past versions. Thus, the citizen is always presented by a clear set of guidelines at every point in time. It will have the side-benefit that many internal contradictions in the law will become self-evident and can be corrected. Again, this is not entirely a new idea, since we already do something similar for important central laws. I am merely asking for this process to be institutionalised and strictly enforced.

Third, the time and date must be mentioned every time a rule or regulation is uploaded or changed. This is very important, because it will tell the citizen when the new law has come into effect. Preferably, the law should come into effect after a few days (say a week) when the change has been notified in order to allow the citizen to comply. The government's software can be easily set up so that officials cannot manipulate the date on which the notice was issued. Note that Wikipedia is again a good model to follow, because it creates a history of each rule and tells us exactly when each change was made.

## ENSHRINED IN AN ACT

Over the last few years, I have discussed the above reforms with politicians, senior bureaucrats and common citizens. No one has yet given me a good counter-argument. The necessary information technology platform is simple. Moreover, it will cost virtually nothing to set up and even less to maintain. In theory, therefore, it could be implemented administratively without an Act but, as we saw with the Right to Information

Act, nothing will change unless it is forced by legislation. Indeed, rent-seekers have every incentive to stall the measures and obfuscate the issue. This is why we need a 'Transparency of Rules' Act—and we could start with just one state.

(This piece was originally published in *Business Standard*, April 2013)

# A FRAMEWORK FOR CREATIVE DESTRUCTION

One of the most important implications of the Complex Adaptive Systems framework is that the world is constantly changing and history can proceed down multiple paths. Applied to the world of business, this means that it is very difficult ex ante to work out precisely how companies will be impacted by technological, economic and policy changes. Even with the best intentions, one should expect business failure as a natural part of innovation and entrepreneurial risk taking. This is the basic idea behind the old Schumpeterian idea of 'creative destruction'. Thus, the lynchpin of a country's economic success is the ability to deal with continuous entry and exit of businesses. However, it was only in 2016 that India finally got a workable framework for this process in the form of the Insolvency and Bankruptcy Code. The following is a brief history of how this important reform came about. It is also a history of how our economic philosophy has changed.

## A PREHISTORY OF IBC

Till 1985, the framework for dealing with corporate insolvency was the Company Act 1956. The law basically left the matter to regular courts and almost no thought was given to critical matters such as super-priority for insolvency costs, choice of liquidators, auction process, financial engineering and so on. The problem was that the law had been framed at a time when corporate failure was not seen as part of the natural creative destruction caused by technological shifts, changes in consumer behaviour, competition and so on. Instead, it was thought that in a rigorously-planned economy, business failures were occasional exceptions caused by deliberate fraud, and perhaps the odd planning failure. The solution was to tighten up planning and licensing, not smoothen out bankruptcy processes.

Individual bankruptcy was dealt under even more archaic laws such as the Presidency Towns Insolvency Act 1909. Again, insolvency was seen as mostly the result of irresponsible behaviour rather than the natural consequence of risk-taking. Presumably this world view parallels that of the early twentieth century's literary image of dissolute sons of zamindars throwing away their family wealth on wine and women. As one can see, mental frameworks of the times have a big impact on the kind of laws that get passed.

By the mid-1980s, it was obvious that something had to be done about the large number of accumulating insolvency cases. The response was the Sick Industrial Companies Act 1985 (SICA) which led to the foundation of the Board of

Industrial and Financial Reconstruction (BIFR). Although the failure of socialist planning should have been obvious by now, there was still a touching belief that insolvent companies could be nursed back to health under the benign watch of the State. Inevitably, BIFR became a warehouse where corporate assets festered for years.

Meanwhile, Section 22 of SICA was regularly misused by unscrupulous promoters to delay enforcement of creditor rights. The passage of the Recovery of Debts Due to Banks and Financial Institutions Act 1993 did not materially change the situation.

## FRAMEWORK FOR CREATIVE DESTRUCTION

The liberalisation of the economy in the 1990s led to a major shift in the mental framework. The economy was now seen as a dynamic system responding to all kinds of changes— technology, domestic policy, international trade and so on. Corporate failure was now seen as part of risk-taking and innovation. The bankruptcy process needed to be a routine mechanism for liquefying economic assets and repurposing them to more efficient uses or competent managers. Moreover, an assertion of creditor rights was seen as key to changing business culture.

The first attempt to incorporate the new thinking was the Securitisation and Reconstruction of Financial Assets and Enforcement of Security Interest Act 2002 (SARFESI). Although SARFESI did lead to some improvements in the recovery process, it dealt only with secured assets and it was soon clear that a more comprehensive framework was needed. A commission led by Justice Srikrishna followed by a committee headed by T.K. Viswanathan looked into the matter. The latter presented a detailed report in 2015 and shortly thereafter a draft bill was presented in parliament. This was how the Insolvency and Bankruptcy Code (IBC) came into being in 2016.

## CLEANING THE BANKS

Even as the government was drafting IBC, it was dealing with a worsening problem—the rapid accumulation of Non-Performing Assets (NPAs) in the banking system, particularly public sector banks. It was the legacy of an unrestrained lending binge from 2006–12. The RBI Governor, Raghuram Rajan responded by pressuring the banks to aggressively recognise problem loans. This meant that problem loans could no longer be routinely rolled over in old-style ever-greening. Second round effects of tightening credit conditions exposed even more stressed assets.

By end 2016, it was clear that a stronger approach was needed to deal with the pile of NPAs. One solution was to create a 'bad bank' where all the NPAs could be housed pending resolution but, there was a concern that it would become a festering warehouse like BIFR. So it was decided to directly use the new IBC framework. The obvious problem was the IBC framework and its institutions like NCLT were brand new and untested.

Fortunately, there was one feature of the NPA problem

that could be exploited—it was concentrated in fifty of the largest cases. The Ministry of Finance and RBI decided that even a new framework should be able to deal with such a small number. In fact, twelve of the largest cases were identified and entered into the IBC process in mid-2017. Some of these large cases used up the 180 plus ninety days mandated under the IBC from May 2018. One of them, Bhushan Steel was sold off for 35,000 crores (plus equity stake). Several others such as, Amtek Auto, Monnet Ispat and Electrosteel followed (these three together collected approximately 12,500 crores). At the time of writing, there was another mega sale being finalised—Essar Steel.

The successful completion of these cases demonstrates that insolvency and bankruptcy is becoming routine in India. Processes, precedents and institutions are getting systematically created. The creditors, meanwhile, are themselves organising an ecosystem of professionals and creditor committees to deal with insolvency. Therefore, India has finally evolved a rule-based framework for risk-taking and creative destruction. This does not mean that things are now flawless but, after seven decades, we have a workable framework that, with continuous improvement, can serve India for generations. This is an important milestone in India's economic history.

# BUILDING A FRAMEWORK FOR POLICY AND GOVERNANCE BASED ON CIVILISATIONAL VALUES

For India to reach its potential, over a billion people need to pull in the same direction and accept far-reaching changes. History suggests that all successful countries have ultimately relied on a common set of civilisational values to underpin mass coordination. What could these shared ideas be in the Indian context?

The current Western model of liberal democracy and open markets has its roots in the intellectual developments triggered by the Calvinist-led Dutch resistance against Spain and the Glorious Revolution of 1688 in England. Under the influence of thinkers like John Locke, the English adopted the Bill of Rights that limited the power of the monarch and guaranteed certain liberties to its citizens. A century later, the ideas of the Enlightenment found their full expression in the US Constitution.

## CULTURE COUNTS

The Western model's success, and the Soviet alternative's collapse, led many to believe that the model was universal. However, the disastrous impact of efforts to impose it on West Asia shows that the model only works in a certain cultural context.

This does not mean there are no alternatives. East Asia has successfully developed using a Confucian approach: the political leadership's main role is to impose order so that the civil service can deliver public services efficiently. Non-democratic China is the obvious example. But it is also true of countries that have democratic institutions such as Japan and Singapore. From a Western perspective, such systems may appear somehow suspect, but these systems have delivered on objectively measurable performance metrics.

Not all political economy systems succeed. But it appears that the ones that do, are deeply rooted in their civilisational values. When India became a Republic in 1950, it adopted formal institutions derived from the West, but also a socialist political economy dominated by a tiny elite and a centralised bureaucracy. Despite its failures, however, the latter arrangement has never been replaced.

What are the values than can build an Indian alternative? We propose four such values that collectively define an internally consistent belief system for a truly Indian State.

Karma: This term tends to be narrowly associated with the theory of reincarnation, but can be more broadly interpreted to mean that every individual is responsible for his actions.

This emphasis on personal responsibility implies a form of individualism but is different from the Western system of rights and entitlements.

Dharma: The word is often narrowly translated to mean religion, but it more broadly means 'to perform one's duty'. Applied to the economic and political sphere, it means that both the citizen and the State are obliged to perform certain duties vis-à-vis each other and society at large. Thus, dharma ties every actor to a web of duties, which are to be carried out irrespective of personal interest (the exact definition of these obligations varies).

Note how Indian thought ties individual responsibility (karma) with wider obligations (dharma). Thus, the Indian ideal falls somewhere between the atomised individualism of Western liberalism and the Confucian hierarchy of social obligations.

Manthan: The Indian, particularly Hindu, worldview is that the world is naturally chaotic as expressed in Shiva's tandava. While other societies try to identify an ideal equilibrium or Utopia and define success in terms of achieving it, Indians see churn as the natural state of the world. The churn releases both negative and positive forces, and success is measured by the ability to absorb the negative and adapt to take advantage of the positive.

The idea of churn and 'creative destruction' is not unique to Indian thought. But it contrasts with the Confucian ideal of static harmony or the end-state Utopia of Marxism. It may explain why Indians have such faith in democracy despite its flaws—it embodies churn within a constitutional framework.

Rule of Law: An important concept in ancient Indian texts is that of matsya nyaya, or Law of the Fish: the big fish eating the small fish. Rule of law and the strict enforcement of contracts are seen as key to avoiding matsya nyaya. Indeed, Indian mythology is full of instances where a promise is shown as sacrosanct even if it is personally costly or unfair. The contrasting conduct of Rama and Krishna in the two epics is a memory of an ancient debate on this issue.

In a constantly churning world, therefore, the role of the State is to create a framework where citizens can take responsibility for their lives and carry out their social obligations. This is neither libertarian nor welfarist. Thus, Kautilya's *Arthashastra* emphasises the role of the State in providing defence, internal security, infrastructure and rule of law, but simultaneously imposes strict limits on the powers of officials who are seen as inherently corruptible. Note the contrast between the strong but limited Kautilyan State and the existing Nehruvian construct of a weak but all-pervasive State.

We are not making the case that India's political economy has generally followed these principles. We merely want to illustrate that it is possible to build an intellectual framework for policy and governance based on our civilisational values. An Indian State rooted in our cultural matrix will be able to better harness the energies of the Indian people.

(This piece was originally published in *The Economic Times*, September 2016, and is credited to the author and Jayant Sinha, the Minister of State for Civil Aviation)